THE SONGS OF SAPPHO

IN ENGLISH TRANSLATION
BY MANY POETS · DECORATED
BY PAUL McPHARLIN
THE PETER PAUPER PRESS
MOUNT VERNON · NEW YORK

SOME NOTES FOR THE GUIDANCE OF THE READER

SAPPHO, one of the earliest and certainly the greatest of Greek lyric poets, was born about 630 B.C. on the island of Lesbos, and lived there most of her life. Lesbos, famous since Homer's day for the beauty of its women and the sweetness of its wine, lies off the coast of Asia Minor (the Lydia of the poems) and is now called Mitylene after its principal city. Not a great deal is known about Sappho's life in Lesbos, except that the ancient story of her unrequited love for Phaon, and her suicide by leaping off the Leucadian cliff, are now considered mythical. So far as modern scholars can surmise, however, she came from a noble and wealthy family, had three brothers, was married, bore at least one child, the daughter Cleis of the poems, was exiled to Syracuse for political reasons, returned after the amnesty of 581 B.C., lived in the satisfying knowledge that she was the bright star of the Aeolian school of poetry, and died at a ripe old age. She apparently was head of a girls' school or women's poetry circle, and probably some of her poems were written as wedding-songs and holiday-festival choruses to be sung by these girls.

FOR many years the standard reading edition of *Sappho* in translation was that of Henry T. Wharton, published first in London, 1877, and since then in several editions there and in New York. The virtue of Wharton's edition for the general reader was that he supplied not only his own literal prose version of each of the poems and fragments, but also the best then-available metrical translations of the principal pieces by others.

A more recent edition of *The Poems of Sappho,* the translations by Edwin Marion Cox, published in a limited edition in London and New York in 1924, makes an excellent supplement to Wharton by giving new prose versions of the same material, as well as excellent metrical versions of many pieces.

But for the modern reader the essential source edition of Sappho is the section devoted to her in the Loeb Classical Library *Lyra Graeca* (volume one) published in 1922 and revised and enlarged in 1928. This book, edited by J. M. Edmonds, and with his excellent prose translations, contains new Sappho discoveries which entirely outweigh in quantity all of her work previously known. This new material is now in a moderately complete condition as the result of scholarly, ingenious and indefatigable work on the part of Edmonds in reconstructing fragmentary manuscripts that had recently been unearthed in Egypt. Some of these reconstructions must remain conjectural, but in the main they seem valid and satisfying.

Edmonds followed the Loeb publication with his *Sappho Revocata*—a limited edition published in London, 1928—which contains the same material with a few additions, but this time mostly in metrical form.

Prose translations by David Moore Robinson (together with metrical versions by Marion Mills Miller) were published in *The Songs of Sappho,* New York, 1925. Particularly valuable to us are Prof. Robinson's translations of the new discoveries and their Edmonds-reconstructions, and the present publishers are appreciative of his permission to reprint them here, together with some of his verse translations from his *Sappho and Her Influence.*

Except for the dropping of many tiny fragments, the present edition gives all of the prose translations of Wharton; all of the prose and most of the metrical translations of Cox; all of the prose and most of the metrical translations of Edmonds; and all of the prose translations by Robinson of the new discoveries. In addition, it follows the example of Wharton in reprinting the best translations in metrical form from other sources—and of course those sources are far richer and more varied than were available to Wharton in 1877.

ALL of Sappho known to us, except the first great hymn to Aphrodite, and a few of the new discoveries which may be complete poems, is fragmentary. Edmonds lists 191 separate pieces, Wharton 170, Cox 130, Robinson 209. Many of these fragments are a word only, or a phrase, which some ancient has preserved for us by quoting; and interesting as these tiny fragments may be to the student of Greek, they are generally valueless—in fact they are irritating—to the general English reader. Therefore in the present edition it has been our policy to eliminate any fragment which in translation lacked either sufficient meaning or sufficient suggestion of poetry to interest that general reader. As a result, the total of our pieces is only 124, but those 124 assay much higher than Edmonds and the others in the specific gravity of poetry.

The present edition takes also one other liberty with the text: whereas Edmonds warns that certain passages are conjectural, by enclosing them in brackets, we have dropped those brackets for the sake of smoother reading and greater poetic enjoyment.

The pieces are numbered consecutively, and follow the order but not the numbers assigned by Edmonds in reconstructing the nine books of Sappho. As a help to the inquiring reader, the number which Edmonds assigns to each piece is given, as are the numbers assigned by Wharton, Cox (who roughly follows Wharton) and Robinson. Where a prose translation by Edmonds is lacking in our text, it is because he used a metrical one in *Lyra Graeca;* where a prose translation by Wharton or Cox is lacking, it is because the piece is one of the recent discoveries, or because one of these two translators made a version almost identical to that of the other.

THE SONGS OF SAPPHO

**THE WORDS I BEGIN ARE WORDS OF AIR
BUT FOR ALL THAT ARE GOOD TO HEAR**

I. TO APHRODITE

APHRODITE splendor-throned immortal, wile-weaving child of Zeus, to thee is my prayer. Whelm not my heart, O Queen, with suffering and sorrow, but come hither I pray thee, if ever ere this thou hast heard and marked my voice afar, and stepping from thy Father's house harnessed a golden chariot, and the strong pinions of thy two swans fair and swift, whirring from heaven through mid-sky, have drawn thee towards the dark earth, and lo! were there; and thou blest Lady, with a smile on that immortal face, didst gently ask what ailed me, and why I called, and what this wild heart would have done, and "Whom shall I make to give thee room in her heart's love, who is it, Sappho, that does thee wrong? For even if she flees thee, she shall soon pursue; if she will not take thy gifts, she yet shall give; and if she loves not, soon love she shall, whether or no";—O come to me now as thou camest then, to assuage my sore trouble and do what my heart would fain have done, thyself my stay in battle.

EDMONDS 1

IMMORTAL Aphrodite of the broidered throne, daughter of Zeus, weaver of wiles, I pray thee break not my spirit with anguish and distress, O Queen. But come hither, if ever before thou didst hear my voice afar, and listen, and leaving thy father's golden house camest with chariot yoked, and fair fleet sparrows drew thee, flapping fast their wings around the dark earth, from heaven through mid sky. Quickly arrived they; and thou, blessèd one, smiling with immortal countenance, didst ask, what now is befallen me, and why now I call, and what I in my mad heart most desire to see. "What Beauty now wouldst thou draw to love thee? Who wrongs thee, Sappho? For even if she flies she shall soon follow, and if she rejects gifts shall yet give, and if she loves not shall soon love, however loth." Come, I pray thee, now too, and release me from cruel cares, and all that my heart desires to accomplish, accomplish thou, and be thyself my ally.

WHARTON 1

IMMORTAL Aphrodite of the shimmering throne, daughter of Zeus, weaver of wiles, I pray thee crush not my spirit with anguish and distress, O Queen. But come hither if ever before thou didst hear my voice afar, and hearken, and leaving the golden house of thy father, camest with chariot yoked, and swift birds drew thee, their swift pinions fluttering over the dark earth, from heaven through mid-space. Quickly they arrived; and thou blessèd one with immortal countenance smiling didst ask: what now is befallen me and why now I call and what I in my heart's madness most desire. "What fair one now would thou draw to love thee? Who wrongs thee Sappho? For even if she flies she shall soon follow, and if she rejects gifts shall soon offer them, and if she loves not shall soon love, however reluctant." Come I pray thee now and release me from cruel cares, and let my heart accomplish all that it desires, and be thou my ally.

COX 1

GLITTERING-THRONED undying Aphrodite,
Wile-weaving daughter of high Zeus, I pray thee
Tame not my soul with heavy woe, dread mistress,
    Nay, nor with anguish,

But hither come, if ever erst of old time
Thou didst incline, and listenedst to my crying,
And from thy father's palace down descending
    Camest with golden

Chariot yoked: thee fair swift flying sparrows
Over dark earth with multitudinous fluttering,
Pinion on pinion through middle ether
    Down from heaven hurried.

Quickly they came like light, and thou, blest lady,
Smiling with clear undying eyes, didst ask me
What was the woe that troubled me, and wherefore
    I had cried to thee;

What thing I longed for to appease my frantic
Soul: and whom now must I persuade, thou askedst,
Whom must entangle to thy love, and who now,
    Sappho, hath wronged thee.

Yea, for if now he shun, he soon shall chase thee;
Yea, if he take not gifts, he soon shall give them;
Yea, if he love not soon shall he begin to
    Love thee, unwilling.

Come to me now too, and from tyrannous sorrow
Free me, and all things that my soul desires to
Have done, do for me Queen, and let thyself too
    Be my great ally.

                      J. ADDINGTON SYMONDS

Beautiful-throned, immortal Aphrodite,
Daughter of Zeus, beguiler, I implore thee,
Weigh me not down with weariness and anguish,
    O thou most holy!

Come to me now, if ever thou in kindness
Hearkenedst my words,—and often hast thou hearkened—
Heeding, and coming from the mansions golden
    Of thy great Father,

Yoking thy chariot, borne by thy most lovely
Consecrated birds, with dusky-tinted pinions,
Waving swift wings from utmost heights of heaven
    Through the mid-ether;

Swiftly they vanished, leaving thee, O goddess,
Smiling, with face immortal in its beauty,
Asking why I grieved, and why in utter longing
    I had dared call thee;

Asking what I sought, thus hopeless in desiring,
Wildered in brain, and spreading nets of passion—
Alas, for whom? and saidst thou, "Who has harmed thee?
    O my poor Sappho!

Though now he flies, erelong he shall pursue thee;
Fearing thy gifts, he too in turn shall bring them;
Loveless to-day, to-morrow he shall woo thee,
    Though thou shouldst spurn him."

Thus seek me now, O holy Aphrodite!
Save me from anguish; give me all I ask for,
Gifts at thy hand; and thine shall be the glory,
    Sacred protector!

                    THOMAS W. HIGGINSON

SHIMMERING-THRONED immortal Aphrodite,
Daughter of Zeus, Enchantress, I implore thee,
Spare me, O Queen, this agony and anguish,
    Crush not my spirit.

Whenever before thou hast hearkened to me—
To my voice calling to thee in the distance,
And heeding, thou hast come, leaving thy father's
    Golden dominions,

With chariot yoked to thy fleet-winged coursers,
Fluttering swift pinions over earth's darkness,
And bringing thee through the infinite, gliding
    Downwards from heaven.

Then, soon they arrived and thou, blessed goddess,
With divine countenance smiling, didst ask me
What new woe had befallen me now and why
    Thus I had called thee,

What in my mad heart was my greatest desire,
Who was it now that must feel my allurements,
Who was the fair one that must be persuaded,
    Who wronged thee Sappho?

For if now she flees, quickly she shall follow
And if she spurns gifts, soon shall she offer them,
Yea, if she knows not love, soon shall she feel it
    Even reluctant.

Come then, I pray, grant me surcease from sorrow,
Drive away care, I beseech thee, O goddess
Fulfill for me what I yearn to accomplish,
    Be thou my ally.

                          EDWIN M. COX

IMMORTAL on thy many-splendored throne
    Hear, Aphrodite Queen, that art
Zeus' witching daughter; and with pain and moan
    break not my heart!
But come, if ever thou hast caught of old
    My distant cry and heard my plea,
And left thy father's palaces of gold
    To visit me;
And yoked thy chariot, and from heaven forth
    Driven thy sparrows fleet and fair
With whirr of wings above the swarthy earth
    Through middle air.
How fast they came! Then, Blessèd One, didst thou
    With lips divinely smiling ask:
"What new mischance is come upon thee now?
    Unto what task
Have I been called? what is the dearest aim
    Of thy mad heart? who is to be
Persuaded to thy passion? Sappho, name
    Thine enemy!
For whoso flies thee now shall soon pursue;
    Who spurns thy gifts shall give anon;
And whoso loves thee not, whate'er she do,
    Shall love thee soon."
Ah, come then, and release me from alarms
    That crush me: all I long to see
Fulfilled, fulfill! A very mate-in-arms
    Be thou to me.

                              WILLIAM MARRIS

II. TO BROCHEO

It is to be a God, methinks, to sit before you and listen close by to the sweet accents and winning laughter which have made the heart in my breast beat fast, I warrant you. When I look on you, Brocheo, my speech comes short or fails me quite, I am tongue-tied; in a moment a delicate fire has overrun my flesh, my eyes grow dim and my ears sing, the sweat runs down me and a trembling takes me altogether, till I am as green and pale as the grass, and death itself seems not very far away;—but now that I am poor, I must fain be content... EDMONDS 2

That man seems to me peer of gods, who sits in thy presence, and hears close to him thy sweet speech and lovely laughter; that indeed makes my heart flutter in my bosom. For when I see thee but a little, I have no utterance left, my tongue is broken down, and straightway a subtle fire has run under my skin, with my eyes I have no sight, my ears ring, sweat bathes me, and a trembling seizes all my body; I am paler than grass, and seem in my madness little better than one dead. But I must dare all, since one so poor . . . WHARTON 2

THAT one seems to me the equal of the gods, who sits in thy presence and hears near him thy sweet voice and lovely laughter; that indeed makes my heart beat fast in my bosom. For when I see thee even a little I am bereft of utterance, my tongue is useless and at once a subtle fire races under my skin, my eyes see nothing, my ears ring, sweat pours forth and all my body is seized with trembling. I am paler than dried grass and seem in my madness little better than dead. But I must dare all . . .
COX 2

PEER of gods he seemeth to me, the blissful
Man who sits and gazes at thee before him,
Close beside thee sits, and in silence hears thee
    Silverly speaking,
Laughing love's low laughter. Oh this, this only
Stirs the troubled heart in my breast to tremble!
For should I but see thee a little moment,
    Straight is my voice hushed;
Yea, my tongue is broken, and through and through me
'Neath the flesh impalpable fire runs tingling;
Nothing see my mine eyes, and a noise of roaring
    Waves in my ear sounds;
Sweat runs down in rivers, a tremor seizes

All my limbs, and paler than grass in autumn,
Caught by pains of menacing death, I falter,
    Lost in the love-trance.
J. ADDINGTON SYMONDS

Peer of the gods, the happiest man I seem
Sitting before thee, rapt at thy sight, hearing
Thy soft laughter and thy voice most gentle,
    Speaking so sweetly.
Then in my bosom my heart wildly flutters,
And, when on thee I gaze never so little,
Bereft am I of all power of utterance,
    My tongue is useless.
There rushes at once through my flesh tingling fire,
My eyes are deprived of all power of vision,
My ears hear nothing but sounds of winds roaring,
    And all is blackness.
Down courses in streams the sweat of emotion,
A dread trembling o'erwhelms me, paler am I
Then dried grass in autumn, and in my madness
    Dead I seem almost.
EDWIN M. COX

Blest beyond earth's bliss, with heaven I deem him
    Blest, the man that in thy presence near thee
Face to face may sit, and while thou speakest,
    Listening may hear thee,
And thy sweet-voiced laughter:—In my bosom
    The rapt heart so troubleth, wildly stirred:
Let me see thee, but a glimpse—and straightway
    Utterance of word

Fails me; no voice comes; my tongue is palsied;
    Thrilling fire through all my flesh hath run;
Mine eyes cannot see, mine ears make dinning
    Noises that stun;
The sweat streameth down, my whole frame seized with
    Shivering,—and wan paleness o'er me spread,
Greener than the grass; I seem with faintness
    Almost as dead.

WALTER HEADLAM

O LIFE divine! to sit before
Thee while thy liquid laughter flows
Melodious, and to listen close
To rippling notes from Love's full score.
O music of thy lovely speech!
My rapid heart beats fast and high,
My tongue-tied soul can only sigh,
And strive for words it cannot reach.
O sudden subtly-running fire!
My ears with dinning ringing sing,
My sight is lost, a blinded thing,
Eyes, hearing, speech, in love expire,
My face pale-green, like wilted grass
Wet by the dew and evening breeze,
Yea, my whole body tremblings seize,
Sweat bathes me, Death nearby doth pass,
Such thrilling swoon, ecstatic death
Is for the gods, but not for me,
My beggar words are naught to thee,
Far-off thy laugh and perfumed breath.

DAVID M. ROBINSON

III. MOONLIGHT

AROUND the fair moon the bright beauty of the stars is lost them when her silver light illumes the world at its fullest. EDMONDS 3

THE stars about the fair moon in their turn hide their bright face when she at about her full lights up all earth with silver. WHARTON 3

THE stars about the fair moon lose their bright beauty when she, almost full, illumines all earth with silver.
COX 4

BRIGHT stars, around the fair Selene peering,
No more their beauty to the night discover
When she, at full, her silver light ensphering,
Floods the world over. T. F. HIGHAM

THE stars around the fair moon fade
Against the night,
When gazing full she fills the glade
And spreads the seas with silvery light.
H. DE VERE STACKPOOLE

THE gleaming stars all about the shining moon
Hide their bright faces, when full-orbed and splendid
In the sky she floats, flooding the shadowed earth with
    Clear silver light. EDWIN M. COX

IV. ORCHARD SONG

... And by the cool waterside the breeze rustles amid the apple-branches, and the quivering leaves shed lethargy ...
EDMONDS 4

And round about the cool water gurgles through apple-boughs, and slumber streams from quivering leaves.
WHARTON 4

And by the cool stream the breeze murmurs through apple branches and slumber pours down from quivering leaves.
COX 5

Cool waters tumble, singing as they go
Through appled boughs. Softly the leaves are dancing.
Down streams a slumber on the drowsy flow,
    My soul entrancing.
T. F. HIGHAM

Through orchard-plots with fragrance crowned
The clear cold fountain murmuring flows;
And forest leaves with rustling sound
Invite to soft repose.
JOHN H. MERIVALE

All around through branches of apple-orchards
Cool streams call, while down from the leaves a-tremble
    Slumber distilleth.
J. ADDINGTON SYMONDS

By the cool water the breeze murmurs, rustling
Through apple branches, while from quivering leaves
    Streams down deep slumber.
EDWIN M. COX

V. TO APHRODITE

... Come, Queen of Love, to bear round golden cups of nectar mingled with gentle cheer unto these comrades of thine and mine.   EDMONDS 6

Come, goddess of Cyprus, and in golden cups serve nectar delicately mixed with delights.   WHARTON 5

    Kupris, hither
Come, and pour from goblets of gold the nectar
Mixed for love's and pleasure's delight with dainty
    Joys of the banquet.   J. ADDINGTON SYMONDS

Come, Venus, come
Hither with thy golden cup,
Where nectar-floated flowerets swim.
Fill, fill the goblet up;
These laughing lips shall kiss the brim—
Come, Venus, come!   ANON.

Goddess of Cyprus come, where beauty lights
The way, and serve in cups of gold these lips
With nectar, mixed by love with all delights
Of golden days, and dusk of amorous nights.
                         H. DE VERE STACKPOOLE

Come hither foam-born Cyprian goddess, come,
And in golden goblets pour richest nectar
All mixed in most ethereal perfection,
    Thus to delight us.   EDWIN M. COX

VI. TO APHRODITE

... And to thee I will burn the rich fat of a white goat ...
                                    EDMONDS 7

But for thee will I lead to the altar the offspring of a white goat ... and add a libation for thee.   WHARTON 7, 8

But for thee I will bring to the altar the young of a white goat ... and add a libation for thee.   COX 8

For thee, unto the altar will I lead
A white goat—
To the altar by the sea:
And there, where waves advance and waves recede,
A full libation will I pour for thee.
H. DE VERE STACKPOOLE

VII. TO APHRODITE

O golden-wreathed Aphrodite, would that such a lot as this were mine . . . ! EDMONDS 9

This lot may I win, golden-crowned Aphrodite.
WHARTON 9

May I win this prize, O golden-crowned Aphrodite.
COX 9

Love-goddess of the wreath of gold,
Would that this lot were mine. J. M. EDMONDS

VIII. TO THE MUSES

. . . Who have made me honored by the gift of their work.
EDMONDS 10

Who gave their gifts and made me honored.
WHARTON 10

. . . Whose gift of their own work
Hath brought me honor. J. M. EDMONDS

IX. TO SOME WEALTHY WOMEN

But I have received true prosperity from the golden Muses, and when I die I shall not be forgot.
EDMONDS 11

    But to me
The Muses gave true wealth, and when I die
I shall not be forgot.
J. M. EDMONDS

X. TO HER COMPANIONS

These songs I will sing right well to-day for the delight of my comrades.
EDMONDS 12

This will I now sing deftly to please my girl-friends.
WHARTON 11

This will I now sing skilfully to please my friends.
COX 11

These songs I'll sing to-day with all my might
For my sweet comrades' sake and dear delight.
J. M. EDMONDS

XI. TO HER FRIENDS

For those I have done good to, do me the greatest wrong.
EDMONDS 13

For they whom I benefit injure me most.   WHARTON 12

For thee to whom I do good, thou harmest me the most.
COX 12

XII. TO HER COMPANIONS

Towards you pretty ones this mind of mine can never change.   EDMONDS 14

To you, fair maidens, my mind does not change.
        COX 14

To you my pretty ones this mind of mine
Can never change.   J. M. EDMONDS

XIII. OF DOVES

And as for them their heart grows light and they slacken the labor of their pinions.   EDMONDS 16

But their heart turned cold and they dropped their wings.
        WHARTON 16

But the spirit within them turned chill and down dropped their wings.   COX 16

XIV. OF CRITICS AND TROUBLE

And as for him who blames me may frenzies and cares seize upon him.   EDMONDS 18

Distress and all care let buffeting winds bear away.
        WHARTON 17

... From my distress: let buffeting winds bear it and all care away.   COX 17

XV. THE DAWN

THE golden slippered Dawn had just come upon me when... EDMONDS 19

ME just now the golden-sandalled Dawn has called.
COX 18

XVI. LYDIAN WORK

... AND a motley gown, a fair Lydian work, reached down to her feet. EDMONDS 20

A BROIDERED strap of beautiful Lydian work covered her feet. WHARTON 19

HER shining ankles clad in fairest fashion
In broidered leather from the realm of Lydia,
    So came the Goddess. COX 20

XVII. OF JASON'S MANTLE

MINGLED with all manner of colors. EDMONDS 21

SHOT with innumerable hues. COX 20

XVIII. TO HECATE

APHRODITE's golden-shining handmaid... EDMONDS 24

THE handmaiden of Aphrodite, shining like gold. COX 54

XIX. MAIDENS

... Rose-armed, saucy-eyed, fair-cheeked, honey-voiced.
EDMONDS 30

With rosy arms and glancing eyes and fair cheeks and honeyed voices.
WHARTON 129

With rosy cheeks and glancing eyes and voices sweet as honey.
COX 118

XX. TO LOVE

Dearest offspring of Earth and Heaven.   EDMONDS 31

Love the child of Aphrodite and Heaven.
WHARTON 132

XXI. TO HESPERUS

Fairest of all the stars that shine.   EDMONDS 32

Thou art, I think, an evening star, of all stars the fairest.
WHARTON 133

XXII. TO PERSUASION

Man-beguiling daughter of Aphrodite.   EDMONDS 33

Persuasion, daughter of Aphrodite.   WHARTON 135

XXIII. TO HER BROTHER CHARAXUS

... WILL give. If you hover about the notable rather than the good and noble, and bid your friends go their ways, and grieve me by saying in your swelling pride that I, forsooth, am become a reproach to you, at such things as these you may rejoice your heart. Feed your fill. For as for me, my mind is not so softly disposed to the anger of a child. But make no mistake in this; the snare never catches the old bird; I know what was the depth of your knavery before, and of what sort is the foe I am opposed to. Be you better advised then, and change your heart; for well I know that being of a gentle disposition I have the Gods on my side.

EDMONDS 35

THOU flittest among men who are notable but neither good nor noble, and thou biddest farewell to thy friends, and grievest me by saying in thy swelling pride of heart that I have become a reproach to thee. Turning to such things mayest thou sate thy heart, for my thought is not so softly disposed towards the anger of children. But do not waver in this: the old bird is not caught by the snare. I understand to what limit of baseness thou formerly didst go, and to what sort of an enemy we have been opposed. But do thou, then, attend to others, and place thy thoughts on better things. For nourishing a contented spirit I clearly know that the blessèd gods are present with me.

ROBINSON 180

AYE, seek the false and shun the true,
And bid your friends go hang for you,
And grieve me in your pride, and say
I bring you shame. Go, have your way,
And flout me till you've had your fill;
I have no fears, and never will,
    For the anger of a child.
Do as you choose; but have a care;
Old birds know how to shun the snare;
The measure of my foe is ta'en;
What once he's done he'll do again;
    I shall not be beguiled.
Be wise in time then, change your heart;
I know the gods will take my part
    Because my spirit's mild.

J. M. EDMONDS

XXIV. TO THE NEREIDS

GOLDEN Nereids, grant me I pray my brother's safe return, and that the true desires of his heart shall be accomplished, and putting away his former errors he shall become a delight to his friends and a grief to his enemies; and may our house be disgraced of no man. And may he be willing to bring honor to his sister; and the sore pain and the words wherewith, in bitter resentment of a taunt that must have cut to the quick, he sought ere he departed to overwhelm my heart, — O, when return he does on some day, may he choose amid his fellow-townsmen's mirth to cast them clean away, and to have a mate, if he desire one, in wedlock due and worthy; and as for thee, thou black and baleful she-dog, thou mayst set that evil snout to the ground and go a-hunting other prey.

EDMONDS 36

[The "black and baleful she-dog" was Doricha, a courtesan beloved by Charaxus in Egypt]

O APHRODITE and ye Nereids, grant me that my brother return hither unharmed, and that whate'er in his heart he wishes come to pass, all shall be completed. And to right all the sins which he formerly committed, and that he prove to be a joy to his friends and a woe to his enemies. And may there come to us no ill fame. May he be willing to make his sister a sharer in his honor; and I will forgive the bitter pain and the words with which formerly he in

his resentment sought to overwhelm my heart when he heard my song that cut to the quick—for amid the merry feast of welcome given him by his fellow citizens when he returns, as I hope he may at no distant day, his it shall be to cast them away; and to find a wife, if he so desires, in worthy wedlock. But as for thee, thou swarthy she-dog, setting thy ill-smelling snout to the ground, pursue other prey.
ROBINSON *183*

Golden Daughters of the Foam
Bring me my brother safely home,
And whatsoe'er his heart desire
Grant he shall possess entire,
And righting what was wrong before,
Shall sorrow his true friends no more,
    That our name bear never a blot.
Then he'll fain his sister to bring
Honor bright; and the bitter sting
And the taunt that made my poor heart sick
When he heard a rebuke such as cuts to the quick—
O soon, when the brimming cup goes round
For his returning safe and sound,
    Shall all that ill be forgot;
And if he's fain of a wife to wed,
Let him take a worthy maid to his bed;
But helly she-dog, as for you,
Ground your ill snout, and game pursue
    Where game is to be got.
J. M. EDMONDS

XXV. TO CHARAXUS

... O Cypris, may she find even thee too bitter, nor boast herself so loud, saying: "What a delightful love-match hath Doricha made this second time!"   EDMONDS 37

... O Cypris, and he found thee more bitter. And the others boasted aloud, saying: "To what a delightful love-match is Doricha come this second time!"

ROBINSON 181

... And, Cypris, may she find e'en Thee
Less sweet than once Thou wert, nor boast what bliss
Is Doricha's with a new mate like this!

J. M. EDMONDS

XXVI. TO ANACTORIA IN LYDIA

The fairest thing in all the world some say is a host of foot, and some again a navy of ships, but to me 'tis the heart's belovèd. And 'tis easy to make this understood by any. Helen, who far surpassed all mankind in beauty, chose for the best of men the destroyer of all the honor of Troy, and thought not so much either of child or parent dear, but was led astray by Love to bestow her heart afar; for woman is ever easy to be bent when she thinks lightly of what is near and dear. See to it then that you remember us Anactoria, now that we are parted from one of whom I would rather the sweet sound of her footfall and the sight of the brightness of her beaming face than all the chariots and armored footmen of Lydia. I know that in this world man cannot have the best; yet to wish that one had a share in what was once shared is better than to forget it. EDMONDS 38

SOME say that the fairest thing upon the dark earth is a host of horsemen, and some say a host of foot soldiers, and others again a fleet of ships, but for me it is my belovèd. And it is easy to make anyone understand this. When Helen saw the most beautiful of mortals, she chose for best that one, the destroyer of all the honor of Troy, and thought not much of child or dear parent, but was led astray by Love, to bestow her heart far off, for woman is ever easy to lead astray when she thinks of no account what is near and dear. Even so, Anactoria, you do not remember, it seems, when she is with you, one the gentle sound of whose footfall I would rather hear and the brightness of whose shining face I would rather see than all the chariots and mail-clad footmen of Lydia. I know that in this world man cannot have the best; yet to pray for a part of what was once shared is better than to forget it . . . COX 3

SOME say an army of horsemen is the fairest thing on the dull black earth, others an army of foot soldiers, and others a navy of ships, but I say 'tis the one with whom one is in love. And it is very easy to make this intelligible to every one. For Helen who saw much beauty of mortals [*or* who far surpassed all in mortal beauty] chose as the

33

noblest [*or* fairest] man the one who quickly destroyed all Troy's honor, and thought not so much either of child or parents dear, but was led astray by Eros to love afar. For the female is always easily bent if one thinks lightly of what is near. And so do thou, Anactoria, now that thou hast gone off to Lydia with a soldier as thy husband, remember us, Sappho and Atthis, though we are not present with thee. I should prefer to see thy lovely step and the bright twinkle of thine eyes than to have all the chariots of the Lydians and all those who fight on foot in arms. ROBINSON 184

A TROOP of horse, the serried ranks of marchers,
A noble fleet, some think these of all on earth
Most beautiful. For me naught else regarding
    Is my beloved.
To understand this is for all most simple,
For thus gazing much on mortal perfection
And knowing already what life could give her,
    Him chose fair Helen,
Him the betrayer of Ilium's honor.
Then recked she not of adored child or parent,
But yielded to love, and forced by her passion,
    Dared Fate in exile.
Thus quickly is bent the will of that woman
To whom things near and dear seem to be nothing.
So mightest thou fail, my Anactoria,
    If she were with you.
She whose gentle footfall and radiant face

Hold the power to charm more than a vision
Of chariots and the mail-clad battalions
    Of Lydia's army.
So must we learn in a world made as this one
Man can never attain his greatest desire,
But must pray for what good fortune Fate holdeth,
    Never unmindful.

EDWIN M. COX

A host of horse or foot may be
To some the fairest sight to see,
To some a fleet of ships; to me
    The loved one passes all.
And easy 'tis to prove my case;
She that had the fairest face
Man ever looked on, set her joy
Upon the ravisher of Troy,
    And heedless of the call
Of parent dear or sweetest child,
Left her home, by Love beguiled
    To give her heart afar.
For ever easy to mislead
Is woman, when she pays no heed
To what is near to her and dear.
Anactory, though far thou'rt gone,
Let us remembered be by one
Whose sweet footfall I'd rather hear,
Whose beaming smile I'd rather see,
Than all the Lydian chariotry
    And mighty men of war.

Well wot I no mortal wight
May have the best for his delight;
Yet a one-time happy lot
Is better longed-for than forgot.   J. M. EDMONDS

XXVII. TO HERA

[Upon Sappho's returning from exile]

MAKE stand beside me in a dream, great Hera, the beauteous shape that appeared in answer to the prayer of the famous kings of Atreus' seed when they had made an end of the overthrow of Troy. At first when they put forth hither from Scamander's swift flood, they could not win home, but ere that could be, were fain to make prayer to thee and to mighty Zeus and to Thyone's lovely child. So now pray I, O Lady, that of thy grace I may do again, as of old, things pure and beautiful among the maids of

Mytilene, whom I have so often taught to dance and to sing upon thy feast-days; and even as Atreus' seed by grace of thee and thy fellow-Gods did put out then from Ilium, so I beseech thee, Hera, aid thou at my prayer this homeward voyage of mine. EDMONDS 40

NEAR me in a dream, O revered Hera, may there be present thy graceful form which in answer to their prayer the Atreidae, the famous kings, saw when they had accomplished the destruction of Troy. At first, when from the swift-flowing Scamander they set forth hither, they were not able to reach home before they had approached with prayer thee and the all-mighty Zeus and Thyone's charming child. So now I beseech thee, revered goddess, that as formerly, I may do again things holy and beautiful among the maidens of Mitylene whom I have taught at thy feasts often to dance and often to sing; and as the Atreidae with your help put out their ships from Ilium, so I urge thee that thou be a helper to me to sail away home, kindly Hera. ROBINSON 196

GREAT Hera, grant my prayer to-night,
And show before my dreaming sight
    The beauteous face
Which Atreus' hero-sons of yore,
When Troy was fall'n and all was o'er,
    Saw of Thy grace,
They that from swift Scamander's flood
Could not win home when out they stood

Till prayer were said to Thee, Great One,
And mighty Zeus and the sweet Son
Thyone bore. So now pray I
To do again things pure and high
The Mytilenian maids among,
The maids I taught with dance and song
    To honor thee;
And even as erst with Your high aid
Atreus' seed the anchor weighed,
So on this homeward way of mine
Be Thy gentle power divine,
    Hera, with me.
J. M. EDMONDS

XXVIII. WHEN TEMPESTS RAGE

WHEN tempests rage, the mariner, for fear of the great blasts of the wind, doth cast his cargo overboard and drive his vessel ashore; as for me, I pray I may be bound nowhither in time of storm, nor be fain with fear lying heavy in my heart to cast my cargo for worthless into the deep; but if so be it should fall to Nereus in his flowing pageant of the sea to receive the gift of my goods ...
EDMONDS 41

IN raging storms sailors in fear of the great winds cast forth their cargoes and beach their ship on the land. May I not sail from anywhere when it is stormy, nor cast all the cargo, worthless and valuable, at random into the deep sea. But if it shall be for Nereus in his flowing procession on the sea to receive my cargo ...
ROBINSON 200

XXIX. LOVE IS IN NO HASTE

... IF my paps could still give suck and my womb were able to bear children, then would I come to another marriage-bed with unfaltering feet; but nay, age now maketh a thousand wrinkles to go upon my flesh, and Love is in no haste to fly to me with his gift of pain ... of the noble ... taking ... O sing us the praises of her of the violet-sweet breast ...

EDMONDS 42

IF my breasts were still capable of giving milk, or my womb could bear children, then would I go to another marriage-couch with feet that tremble not; but, as it is, age already puts about my flesh ten thousand wrinkles, and Eros flies not to me, pursuing me with his gifts of pain ... of the noble ... taking ... O sing us the praises of her of the violet-sweet breast!

ROBINSON 199

AND if these paps their milk could give,
    And this womb make new men live,
Then would I go with footsteps free
    To a bridal bed again;
But now that Age doth spread apace
His thousand wrinkles o'er my face,
Love's in no haste to come to me,
    Love with his gift of pain.

J. M. EDMONDS

XXX. PARTING FROM FRIENDS

And them I answered: "Gentle dames, how you will evermore remember till you be old, our life together in the heyday of youth! For many things did we then together both pure and beautiful. And now that you depart hence, love wrings my heart with very anguish."

EDMONDS 43

To them I said, "Gentle ladies, how ye will remember till old age what we did together in our brilliant youth! For many things holy and beautiful we did then. And now that ye have left the city, love has bitten my heart with keen pangs."

ROBINSON 197

... "Sweet dames," I answered "O,
But you'll remember till you're gray
How we lived in Youth's heyday,
And all that we three used once to do,
And how 'twas good and how 'twas true;
And now that I must part from you
    My lovesick heart's all woe."

J. M. EDMONDS

XXXI. TO HER BELOVED

... For when I look upon you, then meseems Hermione was never such as you are, and just it is to liken you rather to Helen than to a mortal maid; nay, I tell you, I render your beauty the sacrifice of all my thoughts and worship you with all my feelings.

EDMONDS 44

[Hermione was daughter of Helen, and was thus one remove less divine]

Was sick with love ... For when I see thee in my presence, then Hermione appears to me never to have been such as thou art, and to liken thee to golden-haired Helen is reasonable and not to maidens who are mortal; and know this, to thy beauty I render the sacrifices of all my thoughts, and honor thee with all desires.
ROBINSON *193*

> ... For when I look on you,
> Then methinks Hermionè
> Was never such as you to see,
> And I can say with better grace
> That Helen's likeness is in your face
> Than any maiden's of mortal race;
>   Nay, I'd set you higher,
> And to your beauty's altar bring
> All my mind's thought for offering
>   And all my heart's desire.
J. M. EDMONDS

XXXII. TO GONGYLA

Come hither to-night I pray, my rosebud Gongyla, and with your Lydian lyre; surely a desire of my heart ever hovers about your lovely self; for the sight of your very robe thrills me, and I rejoice that it is so. Once on a day,

I too found fault with the Cyprus-born — whose favor I pray these words may lose me not, but rather bring me back again the maiden whom of all womankind I desire the most to see. EDMONDS 45

I BID thee come back the quickest way, my rosebud Gongyla, taking thy milk-white cloak; truly a longing from me flits about thyself, the beautiful, for thy robe sets me all aflutter, as I look at it, and I rejoice. For I myself once blamed the Cyprus-born goddess. I pray that this word lose me not her grace, but bring to me back again thee whom most of all mortal women I desire to see.
ROBINSON 192

COME to-night with your Lydian lyre,
Come, rosebud mine; this heart's desire,
Sweet Gongyla, must go out to you,
For a glimpse of your gown hath thrilled me through
    And put new joy in my heart.
I too found fault once on a day
With the Lady of Love—whose grace I pray
These words of mine may not lose for me,
But bring me a maid I'd rather see
    Than all her kind apart. J. M. EDMONDS

XXXIII. TALK WITH ME

... FOR you came to my house the other day and sang to me, and that is why I am come. O talk with me! come down and make me free of your beauty. For we are walking near, and well you know it. O send your handmaidens away, and may the Gods grant me whatsoever they have for me. Were there a road which man could tread to great Olympus, I would ever . . . EDMONDS 46

INDEED it were nothing unseemly if some blamed thee because thou hast come to me or talked with me, and because thou hast favored so finely those whom it was not fitting; for we walk everywhere. But let us say this, you and me, "Is it possible for mortal maidens to be far away from the women whom they possess and cherish?"
ROBINSON 190

XXXIV. TO A BRIDEGROOM

. . . AND we maidens spend all the night at this door, singing of the love that is between thee, thrice happy bridegroom, and a bride whose breast is sweet as violets. But get thee up and go when the dawn shall come, and may great Hermes lead thy feet where thou shalt find just so much ill-luck as we shall see sleep to-night.
EDMONDS 47

AND we maidens at the doors spend all the night, very happy bridegroom, singing of the love of thee and thy bride with purple girdle . . . But arise when the dawn comes, and go, and may Hermes himself lead thy feet where thou shalt have as much hard luck as we shall see sleep.
ROBINSON 207

XXXV. TO ATTHIS

I LOVED you, Atthis, long ago, when my own girlhood was still all flowers, and you—you seemed to me a small ungainly child.   EDMONDS 48

I LOVED thee once, Atthis, long ago . . . a slight and ill-favored child didst thou seem to me.   WHARTON 33, 34

I LOVED thee Atthis, once long ago . . . to me thou didst seem a small and ungraceful child.   COX 31, 32

I LOVED you, Atthis, once, long long ago . . .
You seemed to me a small, ungainly child.
    C. M. BOWRA

I LOVED you, Atthis, long ago,
While yet my youth was blossoming
And you were still, to outward show,
A slight ungainly little thing.   J. M. EDMONDS

XXXVI. A FOOLISH WOMAN

BUT come, be not so proud of a ring.   EDMONDS 51

FOOLISH woman, pride not thyself on a ring.
    WHARTON 35

FOOLISH woman! Have no pride about a ring.
    COX 33

O FOOLISH woman, dost thou set thy pride upon a ring?
    MICHAEL FIELD

XXXVII. UNDECIDED

I know not what to do; I am in two minds...
EDMONDS 52

I know not what to do; my mind is divided.
WHARTON 36

I know not what to do: I have two minds.
COX 34

In doubt I am, I have two minds,
I know not what to do.
EDWIN M. COX

XXXVIII. THE SKY

I could not expect to touch the sky with my two arms.
EDMONDS 53

I do not think to touch the sky with my two arms.
WHARTON 37

With my two arms, I do not aspire to touch the sky.
COX 35

I think not with these two
White arms to touch the blue.
H. DE VERE STACKPOOLE

XXXIX. LOVE

As for me, love has shaken my wits as a down-rushing whirlwind that falls upon the oaks.
EDMONDS 54

Now Eros shakes my soul, a wind on the mountain falling on the oaks.   WHARTON 42

Now Eros shakes my soul, a wind on the mountain overwhelming the oaks.   COX 40

Lo, Love once more my soul within me rends
Like wind that on the mountain oak descends.
                                          J. ADDINGTON SYMONDS

As wind upon the mountain oaks in storm,
So Eros shakes my soul, my life, my form.
                                          H. DE VERE STACKPOOLE

Now like a mountain wind the oaks o'erwhelming,
Eros shakes my soul.   EDWIN M. COX

Love hath shaken my heart as a down-rushing whirlwind that falleth upon the oaktrees.   J. M. EDMONDS

XL. ON SOFT CUSHIONS

… And I will set you reclining on soft cushions …
                                                        EDMONDS 56

But I upon a soft cushion dispose my limbs.
                                                        WHARTON 50

But upon a soft cushion I dispose my limbs.   COX 46

XLI. GOODNESS IS BEAUTY

He who is fair to look upon is good, and he who is good, will soon be fair also.   WHARTON 101

He that is fair is fair to outward show;
He that is good will soon be fair also.   EDMONDS 58

He who is fair is good to look upon;
He who is good is fair, though youth be gone.
    H. DE VERE STACKPOOLE

He should be good who is fair of face,
And he will be fair whose soul has grace.
    EDWIN M. COX

Beauty, fair flower, upon the surface lies;
But Worth with Beauty soon in aspect vies.   ANON.

XLII. FAR SWEETER

Far sweeter-tunèd than the lyre . . . more golden than gold.   EDMONDS 59, 60

Far sweeter of tone than harp, more golden than gold.
    WHARTON 122, 123

Than the lyre, far sweeter in tone, than gold, more golden.   COX 115

Far sweeter than the throbbing lyre in sound,
A voice more golden than gold, new found.
    EDWIN M. COX

XLIII. FROM A WEDDING SONG

. . . But come, dear maidens, let us end our song, for day is at hand.   EDMONDS 65

But come, dear girls, let us cease from our song; for the day is near.   ROBINSON 206

XLIV. THE WEDDING OF ANDROMACHE

... Cyprus ... came a herald sped by the might of his swift legs bringing speedily these fair tidings unto the people of Ida.... and throughout the rest of Asia these tidings won a fame that never died: "Hector and his comrades bring from sacred Thebe and fair-flowing Placia, by ship upon the briny sea, the dainty Andromache of the glancing eye; and many are the golden bracelets and the purple robes which the wind is bringing, indeed a richly-varied bride-gift; and without number also are the silver goblets and the ornaments of ivory." So spake the herald; and Hector's dear father leapt up in haste, and the news went forth through Ilus' spacious city. Straightway the children of Ilus harnessed the mules to the wheelèd cars, and the whole throng of the women and of the dainty-ankled maidens mounted therein, the daughters of Priam riding apart; and the men did harness horses to the chariots, and the young men went with them one and all; till a mighty people moved mightily along, and the drivers drove their boss-bedizened steeds out of the city...... Then, when the godlike Hector and Andromache were mounted in the chariots, they accompanied them in one throng, and the city sped back into lovely Ilium. The sweet-toned flute and the lyre were mingled with the sound of the rattle, aye, and the maidens sang clear and well a holy song, till a marvelous great sound rose to the sky and the Gods in heaven laughed. Everywhere in the ways was festal mirth; for bowls and cups were mixed, and myrrh and cassia and frankincense curled aloft. Meanwhile the elder women raised a loud cry, and all the men shouted amain a delightful song of thanksgiving unto the Far-Darting God of the lyre, and hymned the praise of the god-like Hector and Andromache.

EDMONDS 66

... CYPRUS ... a herald came sustained by the might of his swift limbs, to the folk of Ida these fair tidings bringing as a swift messenger ... and throughout the rest of Asia these tidings were a fame that never since has died. "Hector and his mates are bringing from holy Thebe and ever-flowing Placia the shyly-glancing lovely Andromache in ships upon the briny sea; and many bracelets of gold and robes of purple, yes and smooth rich embroideries, varied bridal dower, and silver beakers beyond number, and ivories." So he spoke; and quickly uprose the father beloved, and rumor went throughout the widewayed city of Ilus. Straightway the people of Ilium under the well-wheeled carts brought the mules, and thereon mounted all the throng of wives and virgins of slender ankles; but apart from them Priam's daughters went. And steeds the men brought under the chariots, and with them went all the youths. And mightily moved the mighty people, and charioteers brought out their colts adorned with embossed cheek-pieces. ... When then on their cars they were mounted, like to gods, Hector and Andromache, there drove with them all the Trojan men and Trojan women into delightful Ilium ... they mingled ... and as the maidens ... and cassia and incense flamed up in smoke. And the wives, those who were older, cried aloud, and all the men shouted in a strong clear voice a lovely paean, calling on the name of the Far-Darter of the goodly lyre, and they hymned Hector and Andromache, like to the gods.

ROBINSON 208

"Hector and his men bring the girl, her eyes gleaming,
From Thebe the Holy, from Placia fount unfailing,
Andromache the beautiful, over the salt sea sailing
With whorls and roundlets golden, with robes for her arraying
Purple embroidered daintily, away on the wind streaming;
And silver cups uncountable and carven ivory."
    This was the herald's story.
And Hector's father heard it, and gay he rose, and the saying
Went the round of Troy Town for all friends' knowing.
Then the men of Troy put their mules into harnessing
Back against the chariots, and then mounted pressing
The rout of young women, and of lightfoot girls going,
Then Priam's daughters apart; and then the soldiers
Were harnessing their horses under the chariot rim,
The young men in their prime. ....
And the sweet piping with lyreplay was blending,
With castanets clashing; and the maidens high singing
Sang the holy song to heaven ascending
With strange din ringing. ....
There were myrrh and cassia with frankincense smoking;
There the elder women their chant were choiring;

There all the men sang their high song invoking
The God far-darting, Paean of the lyring,
Singing for Hector and for Andromache divine.

GEORGE ALLEN

. . . With tidings fair to Ida's people, sped
By strength of fleet limb, swift a herald came,
And Asia through, this news won living fame:—
"Hector and all his meinie hither bring,
From sacred Thebè and the fair-flowing
Placia, on shipboard o'er the briny sea
The dainty sparkling-eyed Andromache;
Armlets of gold come plenty down the wind
And purple find, bridegifts of every kind,
Much ivory too, and many a silver cup."
    He spake, and Hector's father dear leapt up,
And quick the news went Troy's wide ways about.
Eftsoons her sons the wheelèd wains brought out
And yoked the mules, and in the dames all stept
And damsels slender-ankled, one wain kept
Apart for Priam's daughters; every man
Joined horse to chariot-pole, and with them ran
The striplings each and all,—till in one throng
A mighty folk went mightily along.
    The drivers drave the boss-bedizened steeds
Out of the city . . . . . .
    When in their equipage the godlike pair,
Andromache and Hector, mounted were,

Thousands convoyed them as the town sped home
Towards the walls of lovely Ilium;
Sweet-tunèd flute was mingled with the lyre
To the din of rattles, and a maiden quire
Shrilled holy song, till wide the sky was riven
With wondrous sound, and the Gods laughed
    in Heaven.
In every street was merrymaking; mixt
Were wine-bowl and wine-cup; and the firm-fixt
Altars sent curling upward to the skies
Frankincense, myrrh, and cassia, 'mid the cries
Of the elder women, while the men each one
The Paean sweet sang loud to Leto's Son,
Lord of the Lyre and Bow, and hymned in glee
The godlike Hector and Andromache.

J. M. EDMONDS

XLV. GARLANDS

AND the maids ripe for wedlock wove garlands.

EDMONDS 67

BUT in their time they plaited garlands.   WHARTON 73

THEY plaited garlands in their time.   MICHAEL FIELD

XLVI. TO THE GRACES

HITHER, pure rose-armed Graces, daughters of Zeus.

EDMONDS 68

Come, rosy-armed pure Graces, daughters of Zeus.
WHARTON 65

Come, rosy-armed Graces, virgin daughters of Zeus.
COX 62

Ye rosy-armed, pure Graces, come,
Daughters of Zeus, be near!   MICHAEL FIELD

XLVII. THE GOD OF LOVE

... Come from heaven and throw off his purple mantle.
EDMONDS 69

Coming from heaven wearing a purple mantle.
WHARTON 64

Coming from heaven, clad in a purple mantle.   COX 61

    From heaven he came,
And round him the red chlamys burned like flame.
J. ADDINGTON SYMONDS

From heaven returning; red of hue,
His chlamys burning against the blue.
H. DE VERE STACKPOOLE

XLVIII. TO AN UNEDUCATED WOMAN

When you are dead you will lie unremembered for evermore; for you have no part in the roses that come from

Pieria; nay, obscure here, you will move obscure from the house of Death, and flit to and fro among such of the dead as have no fame. EDMONDS 71

BUT thou shalt lie dead, nor shall there ever be any remembrance of thee then or thereafter, for thou hast not of the roses of Pieria; but thou shalt wander obscure even in the house of Hades, flitting among the shadowy dead.
WHARTON 68

BUT thou shalt ever lie dead nor shall there be any remembrance of thee then or ever, for thou hast none of the roses of Pieria; but thou shalt wander unnoticed, even in the houses of Hades flitting among the shadowy dead.
COX 65

FOREVER shalt thou lie dead, nor shall there be any remembrance of thee now or hereafter, for never hast thou had any of the roses of Pieria; but thou shalt wander, eternally unregarded in the houses of Hades, flitting among the insubstantial shades. COX 65

THOU liest dead, and there will be no memory left behind
Of thee or thine in all the earth, for never didst thou bind
The roses of Pierian streams upon thy brow; thy doom
Is now to flit with unknown ghosts in cold and nameless
    gloom. EDWIN ARNOLD

>Yea, thou shalt die,
>And lie
>   Dumb in the silent tomb;
>Nor of thy name
>Shall there be any fame
>   In ages yet to be or years to come:
>For of the flowering Rose
>Which on Pieria blows,
>   Thou hast no share:
>But in sad Hades' house,
>Unknown, inglorious
>'Mid the dim shades that wander there
>Shalt thou flit forth and haunt the filmy air.

J. ADDINGTON SYMONDS

>Dead shalt thou lie; and nought
>Be told of thee or thought,
>For thou hast plucked not of the Muses' tree:
>   And even in Hades' halls
>   Amidst thy fellow-thralls
>No friendly shade thy shade shall company!

THOMAS HARDY

>Thee too the years shall cover; thou shalt be
>As the rose born of one same blood with thee,
>As a song sung, as a word said, and fall
>Flower-wise, and be not any more at all,
>Nor any memory of thee anywhere;
>For never Muse has bound above thine hair

The high Pierian flowers whose graft outgrows
All summer kinship of the mortal rose
And color of deciduous days, nor shed
Reflex and flush of heaven about thine head...
      ALGERNON C. SWINBURNE

Dead shalt thou lie for ever, and forgotten,
For whom the flowers of song have never bloomed;
A wanderer amidst the unbegotten,
In Hades' house a shadow aye entombed.
      H. DE VERE STACKPOOLE

XLIX. NO MAIDEN

I do not believe that any maiden that shall see the sunlight will ever rival you in your art....   EDMONDS 72

No one maiden I think shall at any time see the sunlight that shall be as wise as thou.   WHARTON 69

I think that no maiden shall ever see the sunlight, who shall have thy wisdom.   COX 66

No maiden, I think, more wise than thou
Shall ever see the sun.   EDWIN M. COX

Never on any maiden, the golden sun shall shine,
Never on any maiden whose wisdom matches thine.
      H. DE VERE STACKPOOLE

57

L. HERO OF GYARA

WELL did I teach Hero of Gyara, the fleetly-running maid...   EDMONDS 73

I TAUGHT Hero of Gyara, the swift runner.   WHARTON 71

HERO of Gyara, that swift runner, I taught.   COX 68

LI. NO REVENGE

... YET I am not resentful in spirit, but have the heart of a little child.   EDMONDS 74

I AM not one of revengeful temper, but have a simple mind.   WHARTON 72

I AM not of a malign nature but have a calm temper.
   COX 69

LII. MY SERVITOR LOVE

MY servitor Love and thou, O Sappho...   EDMONDS 75

THOU and my servant Love.   WHARTON 74

LIII. FAME

SOMEBODY, I tell you, will remember us hereafter ... others have been disappointed by oblivion, but never one by the judgment of good men.   EDMONDS 76, 77

MEN I think will remember us even hereafter.
                                    WHARTON 32

METHINKS hereafter in some later spring
Echo will bear to men the songs we sing.
                          H. DE VERE STACKPOOLE

LIV. TO HER LUTE

UP, my lute divine, and make thyself a thing of speech...
                                    EDMONDS 80

COME now, divine shell, become vocal for me.
                                    WHARTON 45

COME, O divine shell, yield thy resonances to me.
                                         COX 42

COME now, divine tortoise, mayest thou become endowed
with speech for me.   ROBINSON 58

COME, make thyself a thing of speech,
      My Lute divine.   J. M. EDMONDS

COME, O come, divinest shell,
And in my ear all thy secrets tell.   EDWIN M. COX

SINGING, O shell, divine!
Let now thy voice be mine.   H. DE VERE STACKPOOLE

LV. TO ATTHIS

Lo! Love the looser of limbs stirs me, that creature irresistible, bitter-sweet; but you, Atthis, have come to hate the thought of me, and run after Andromeda in my stead.
EDMONDS 81

Now Love masters my limbs and shakes me, fatal creature, bitter-sweet . . . but to thee, Atthis, the thought of me is hateful; thou flittest to Andromeda.
WHARTON 40, 41

Now Love the limb-loosener sweeps me away in his eddy, a sweet though bitter irresistible beast. . . . Yet, Atthis, it is hateful to thee to think of me, and thou flittest to Andromeda.
ROBINSON 7, 8

Love has unbound my limbs and set me shaking,
A monster bitter-sweet and my unmaking.
C. M. BOWRA

Now Love, the ineluctable, with bitter sweetness
Fills me, overwhelms me, and shakes my being.
EDWIN M. COX

Lo, Love once more, the limb-dissolving King,
The bitter-sweet impracticable thing,
Wild-beast-like rends me with fierce quivering.
J. ADDINGTON SYMONDS

The Looser of our Limbs shakes me amain,
Love, the resistless ravener, joy-in-pain;
But, Atthis, love is turned to hate in thee;
Andromeda's thy quest instead of me.
> J. M. EDMONDS

Now Love has bound me, trembling, hands and feet,
O Love so fatal, Love so bitter-sweet.
Hateful my face is to thee,
Hateful to thee beyond speaking,
Atthis, who fliest from me
Like a white bird Andromeda seeking.
> H. DE VERE STACKPOOLE

LVI. TO ATTHIS

" . . . Sappho, I swear if you come not forth I will love you no more. O rise and shine upon us and set free your beloved strength from the bed, and then like a pure lily beside the spring hold aloof your Chian robe and wash you in the water. And Cleis shall bring down from your presses saffron smock and purple robe; and let a mantle be put over you and crowned with a wreath of flowers tied about your head; and so come, sweet with all the beauty with which you make me mad. And do you, Praxinoë roast us nuts, so that I may make the maidens a sweeter breakfast; for one of the Gods, child, has vouchsafed us a boon. This very day has Sappho the fairest of all women vowed that she will surely return with us, the mother with her children." . . . Dearest Atthis, can you then forget all this that happened in the old days? . . . EDMONDS 82

"Sappho, truly unless thou wilt rise and come out, I shall not love thee. Oh, rise and show thyself to us, and from thy bed release thy beloved strength, and with water like a pure lily beside the spring wash thee, tucking up thy Chian robe. And Cleis shall cast upon thee from thy press saffron smock and purple robe. Put a mantle over thee, and let wreaths of flowers bound about thy head crown thee; and so come, sweet with the beauty with which thou makest me mad. Roast us nuts, O Praxinoë, so that I may make the maidens a sweeter breakfast drink. For these things come to us from one of the gods, child. This very day Sappho, the fairest of women, vowed that she would return to Mitylene, most beloved of cities. Return with us, the mother with her brood." Dearest Atthis, dost thou forget all those things of the past, or dost thou still remember? ROBINSON 188

... "Sappho, if you say me nay
My love is lost you from this day.
O quit your bed, sweet star of mine,
Rise in your dear strength and shine,
And like a lily pure as snow
Standing by the water's flow,
Tuck up your smock of Chian seam
And stand and wash you in the stream.
Then shall Cleis from the press
Take and give you for your dress
Shift of saffron, robe of red,
Cloak for shoulders, wreath for head,
And you shall come in all the grace
That makes me wild to see your face.
Go roast me nuts, Praxinoë,
That each maid's breakfast merrier be;
For God has sent us luck this morn;
'Tis the day our Sappho's sworn
That she, the loveliest woman known,
At Mytilen, the dearest town,
Shall give her children back their own."
   Dearest Atthis, dearest yet,
Can it be that you forget? J. M. EDMONDS

LVII. TO ATTHIS LEAVING

So I shall never see Atthis more, and in sooth I might as well be dead. And yet she wept full sore to leave me behind and said "Alas! how sad our lot; Sappho, I swear 'tis all against my will I leave thee"; and I answered her, "Go your way rejoicing and remember me, for you know I doted upon you. And if you remember not, O then I will remind you of what you forget, how dear and beautiful was the life we led together. For with many a garland of violets and sweet roses mingled you have decked your flowing locks by my side, and with many a woven necklet made of a hundred blossoms your dainty throat; and with unguent in plenty, both of the precious and the royal, have you anointed your fair young skin in my bosom, and upon a soft couch had from the hands of gentle serving-maids all that a delicate-living Ionian could desire; and no hill was there, nor holy place nor waterbrook, whither we did not go, nor ever did the crowded noise of the early Spring fill any wood with the medley-song of nightingales, but you wandered thither with me..."
                                                                EDMONDS 83

I shall never see Atthis again, and I surely wish I were dead. Yet she wept much when she left me, and said this to me, "Woe is me, how terribly we have suffered! Sappho truly against my will I leave thee." And I answered her with these words, "Rejoicing go thy way, and remember me; for thou knowest how I loved thee. But if it be not so, I am fain to remind thee of what thou hast forgot, those many dear and beautiful experiences we had together. For with many wreaths of violets and sweet roses thou hast bound my tresses by my side, and many woven chains entwined of a hundred flowers thou hast put about my tender neck; and with many a vase of costly and royal myrrh hast thou anointed my soft skin; and, reclining with me upon the couch, hast taken all thy fill of dainty meats and of sweet drinks . . . "   ROBINSON 191

I NE'ER shall see my Atthis more,
And sure 'tis dead that I well might be;
And yet as she went she wept full sore
And cried "Alack and woe is me!
    God knows 'tis not that I would."
And I said "Good speed, and forget me never,
I wot you know how I loved you ever.
But if so be that you know it not,
I'll e'en tell all that you've forgot
    Of those days so dear and good,
And how many wreaths of the violet
And the sweet sweet rose together met
    You've bound about your hair,
And round your pretty throat how plenty
Chains of a hundred flowers and twenty,
And phials how often from my chest
Of balm the best and costliest
You've poured on your bosom fair.
And cushioned soft, from cup and dish,
Of all Ionian taste could wish

>   Or handmaids trim supply
> You've had your fill; mount, sacred spot,
> Brookside, there's none we haunted not;
> No grove was loud at break of Spring
> With nightingales' sweet jargoning
>   But we went there, you and I . . ."

J. M. EDMONDS

>   TRULY I want to die,
> Such was her weeping when she said good-bye.
>   These words she said to me:
>   "What sad calamity!
> Sappho, I leave you most unwillingly."
>   To her I made reply:
>   "Go with good heart, but try
> Not to forget our love in days gone by.
>   Else let me call to mind,
>   If your heart proves unkind,
> The soft delightful ways you leave behind.
>   Many a coronet
>   Of rose and violet,
> Crocus and dill upon your brow you set:
>   Many a necklace too
>   Round your soft throat you threw,
> Woven with me from buds of ravishing hue,
>   And often balm you spread
>   Of myrrh upon my head,
> And royal ointment on my hair you shed."

C. M. BOWRA

LVIII. TO A VIRGIN

... AND I answered you, "I swear to you by the Goddess that although I, like you, had of Zeus but one virginity, nevertheless I feared not the threshold beyond which Hera had bidden me cast it away." Aye, thus I heartened you, and cried aloud, "That night was sweet enough for me, neither have you, dear maid, anything to fear." ... Nay, I tell you, I prayed that night of ours might be made twice as long. EDMONDS 84

... AND I answered thee thus: "I have sworn this to thee by the Goddess Aphrodite that, although I myself, too, had from Zeus not many virginities, but one, nevertheless I feared not the threshold beyond which Hera had commanded me to cast it away." With these words I cheered thee, and shouted aloud, "To me, virgin, the night did not appear to be heavy, so that thou too need not be distraught with fear." ROBINSON 186

LIX. A DREAM OF HERMES
[Who led the dead to Hades]

... "SURELY," said Gongyla, "you cannot tell? or have your eyes seen a sign?" "They have," said I; "Hermes came to me in a dream, and I said—O Master, I am altogether undone; for by the Blessed Goddess I swear to thee I care not so much any more that I am exalted unto prosperity, but a desire possesses me to die, and to behold the dewy lotus-bearing banks of Acheron...." EDMONDS 85

"Long," said I, "it cannot be." And Gongyla said, "How knowest thou that? Surely not! Or what sign art thou willing to show thy children?" "Certainly, I'll tell you," I answered. "Hermes came in, and looking upon him I said, O Master, we are utterly lost. For I swear by the blessèd mistress Aphrodite that I care naught any more that I have been lifted up to prosperity, but a longing to die hath seized me. I desire thee to set me in the dewy field whither in former days thou didst lead Atreus' son Agamemnon and all the select flower of the Achaeans. But I must leave this light of day, seeing that I . . ."

ROBINSON 204

"Long" said I "it cannot be."
"How know you that?" asked Gongylè;
"Has sign been sent you?" "Yes" I said;
"Great Hermes stood before my bed,
    And Lord Most High I cried to him,
    My joys are done;
All my great prosperity,
So help me Love! is nought to me;
My one desire's to die, and see
    The dew-besprinkled lotus-brim
    Of Acheron . . ."

J. M. EDMONDS

LX. ON ANACTORIA

ATTHIS, our belovèd Anactoria dwells in far-off Sardis, but she often sends her thoughts hither, thinking how once we used to live in the days when you were like a glorious Goddess to her and she loved your song the best. And now she shines among the dames of Lydia as after sunset the rosy-fingered Moon beside the stars that are about her, when she spreads her light o'er briny sea and eke o'er flowery field, while the dew lies so far on the ground and the roses revive and the dainty anthrysc and the melilot with all its blooms. And oftentime while our belovèd wanders abroad, when she calls to mind the love of gentle Atthis, her tender breast, for sure, is weighed down deep with longing; and she cries aloud for us to come thither; and what she says we know full well, you and I, for flower-tressèd Night that hath the many ears calls it to us along all that lies between. EDMONDS *86*

ATTHIS, Anactoria dear to you and dear to me, is dwelling in distant Sardis, often turning her thought hither, thinking how once we lived together a life in which she held thee like to a glorious goddess, and took especial delight in thy song. And now she is conspicuous among the Lydian dames as, when the sun has set, is the rosy-fingered moon beside the stars about her, when she spreads her light o'er briny sea and o'er the many-flowered fields, while the noble dew is shed forth, and the roses revive and the dainty anthrysc and the honey-lotus with its bloom. And ofttimes as she wanders about, thinking of her love for gentle Atthis, doubtless her tender heart is weighted down with longing; and she cries shrilly to us to come thither; and what she says, not unknown to us, Night, the many-eared, calls to us across the severing sea. ROBINSON *187*

ATTHIS, our Anactory,
Dear to you and dear to me,
 Is in far Sardis dwelling;
But her thoughts turn often hither
To the life we led together,
When you her earthly Goddess were,
Passing noble, passing fair,
 Your song all song excelling.
Now the Lydian dames beside
She's like the Moon at eventide
With her rosy fingers red
Shining, when the Sun's abed,
 Beside her neighbor fires,
And launching light o'er briny sea
And eke o'er blossom-broidered lea,
While the dew its boon outsheds
And pinks and roses lift their heads
 And gilliflowers their spires.
And often as her way she wanders
And on gentle Atthis ponders,
With sad longing love oppressed
Her heart sinks in her tender breast
 Till she cries in pain
"O come to me!"—for you and I
Know the burden of her cry,
Since flower-robed Night of the myriad ears
Sends us word of what she hears
 Across the severing main.

J. M. EDMONDS

ATTHIS, in Sardis far away
    Anactoria dear to thee
    And dear indeed alike to me
Now dwells, but hither often stray

Her thoughts sent usward by the power
    That lives anew the life she loved
    When thou her glorious goddess proved,—
Thy songs her joy at every hour.

You were her sun, now set too soon;
    Among the Lydian dames she shines
    As, after sunset, glow the lines
Of light the rosy-fingered moon

Throws on her retinue of stars
    Spreading a far-flung lane of beams
    That gleams the salt sea o'er and streams
Across the rocky shore that bars

In vain the light that floods its gloom,
    And leaping landward bathes the fields
    Where many a flower its beauty yields
With fragrant variegated bloom.

Full fair the dew springs forth and holds
    The light, the roses lift their heads,
    The dainty anthryscs quit their beds,
The clover, honey-rich, unfolds.

Through all this beauty, hard unrest
    And longing crushing like a stone
    Her tender heart, ofttimes alone
She wanders with a weighted breast.

She cannot calm her quivering lip
    And through the balmy, scented dark
    She cries aloud we must embark
And thither come on some swift ship.

Full clear her words to thee and me,
    For night with all her many ears
    Their ardent sound full gladly hears
And sends us o'er the severing sea.

                        DAVID M. ROBINSON

A GLORIOUS goddess in her eyes
Were you, her comrade, and your songs
Above all other songs she'd prize.
With Lydian women now she dwells
Surpassing them, as when day dies
The rosy-fingered moon excels
The host of stars, and light illumes
The salt sea and the cornland glows
With light upon its thousand blooms.
In loveliness the dew spills over
And with new strength revives the rose,
Slim grasses and the flowering clover.
But sadly up and down she goes,
Remembering Atthis, once her lover.
And in her heart sick longing grows.

                        C. M. BOWRA

LXI. TO HERSELF

Be still, my Soul; not thus for me,
With thoughts outwelling glib and free,
    Canst thou effuse
Adonis-hymns whose harmony
    Shall please the Muse.
Such thoughts Desire that doth make fame cleap
And Love that doth hearts in bondage keep
    Away have driven;
And Persuasion's whelm-wit vial of gold
To thy fancy's lip the sweets doth hold
    Of the wine of Heaven.   EDMONDS 86B

LXII. TO APHRODITE

... And hanging on either side thy face the purple handkerchief which Timas sent for thee from Phocaea, a precious gift from a precious giver ...   EDMONDS 87

And purple napkins for thy lap .... (even these wilt thou despise) I sent from Phocaea, precious gifts for thy lap.
    WHARTON 44

And tying the snood of cramoisie
    To hang beside Thy face,
The precious gift that came to Thee
From a precious giver o'er the sea
    Thy cheeks to grace.   J. M. EDMONDS

LXIII. TO ATTHIS

You are come; it is well; I was longing for you, and now you have made my heart to flame up and burn with love. Bless you, I say, thrice bless you, and for just so long as you and I have been parted.   EDMONDS 89

Thou hast come: thou hast done well. I longed for thee: and thou hast inflamed my heart already burning with desire. Hail to us, many times hail, and for as long as we were parted from one another.   ROBINSON 15

You are come; 'tis well; I longed for you;
And you have brought to flame anew
    The fire of love in my heart;
Welcome's the burden of my song
And blessings on you for just so long
    As you and I were apart.   J. M. EDMONDS

LXIV. BRILLIANCE

... A GLAMOR blinding the eyes ...   EDMONDS 90

A SHEEN blinding the eyes like to the hyacinth-flower.
    ROBINSON 122

LXV. DEATH

DEATH is an ill; the gods at least think so,
Or else themselves had perished long ago.   EDMONDS 91

DEATH is evil; the gods have so judged: had it been good,
they would die.   WHARTON 137

DEATH is an evil, for the gods choose breath;
Had Death been good the gods had chosen Death.
    H. DE VERE STACKPOOLE

To die must needs be sad, the gods do know it;
For were death sweet, they'd die, and straightway show it.
    EDWIN ARNOLD

LXVI. A PUBLIC BEAUTY

... With whom you are mingled in a vagrant friendship which deems that beautiful which any man may have for the asking.   EDMONDS 92

[Perhaps referring to her brother's love for Doricha]

Which deems that beautiful which is devoted to the public good.   ROBINSON 162

LXVII. STUBBORNNESS

Foolish girl, do not try to bend a stubborn heart.
   EDMONDS 93

Fool, faint not thou in thy strong heart.   WHARTON 110

LXVIII. OF THE CRICKET

... And pours down a sweet shrill song from beneath his wings, when the Sun-god illumines the earth with his down-shed flame outspread ...   EDMONDS 94

From beneath her wings she pours forth a clear shrill song, when she shouts down the outspread perpendicular blaze of the noonday sun.   ROBINSON 96

... AND sings
A shrill sweet song from 'neath her wings,
When the Sun his rays doth spread
Plumb from the zenith ... J. M. EDMONDS

LXIX. I HAVE COME BACK

DAINTY one, to thee from whom I had been parted altogether I have come back again ... EDMONDS 96

Lo! to the soft arms of her whom I had shunned so long I have come back. ROBINSON 121

FAIR one, from whom I'd parted been
So long and far, lo, I behold you ... J. M. EDMONDS

LXX. LEDA

THEY say that once upon a time Leda found hidden an egg of hyacinthine hue ... EDMONDS 97

LEDA they say once found an egg hidden under hyacinth-blossoms. WHARTON 56

THEY say that Leda once found an egg under the hyacinths. COX 52

THEY say, 'neath leaf and blossom
Leda found in the gloom
An egg, white as her bosom,
Under an iris bloom. H. DE VERE STACKPOOLE

LXXI. THE COUNTRY GIRL

. . . And what countrified wench in countrified clothes fires your breast, though she knows not how to draw her gown over her ankles?   EDMONDS 98

What peasant-girl bewitches thy heart, who knows not how to draw her dress about her ankles?   WHARTON 70

What country maiden charms thy heart,
However fair, however sweet,
Who has not learned by gracious Art
To draw her dress around her feet?
   H. DE VERE STACKPOOLE

What rustic girl bewitches thee,
Who cannot even draw
Her garments neat as they should be,
Her ankles roundabout?   EDWIN M. COX

LXXII. THE YOUNG HUSBAND

. . . But if you love me, choose yourself a younger wife; for I cannot submit to live with one that is younger than I.   EDMONDS 99

But if thou lovest us, choose a younger bed-fellow; for I will not brook to live with thee, thine elder as I am.   WHARTON 75

For if thou lovest us, choose another and a younger spouse;
for I will not endure to live with thee, old woman with
young man. COX 72

If love thou hast for me, not hate,
Arise and find a younger mate;
For I no longer will abide
Where youth and age lie side by side.
H. DE VERE STACKPOOLE

LXXIII. WEALTH AND WORTH

Wealth without worth is no harmless housemate; but
the blending of the two is the top of fortune.
EDMONDS 100

Wealth without worth is no safe neighbor but the mixture of both is the height of happiness. WHARTON 81

Wealth without thee, Worthiness, is no safe neighbor,
but the mixture of both is the height of happiness.
COX 78

Wealth without Worth is a dangerous guest;
They that have both are of all men most blest.
J. M. EDMONDS

Wealth without virtue is a dangerous guest;
Who holds them mingled is supremely blest.
JOHN H. MERIVALE

LXXIV. COME, GRACES

O hither, soft Graces and lovely-tressèd Muses.
EDMONDS 101

Come now, delicate Graces and fair-haired Muses.
WHARTON 60

Come, Graces soft and Muses lovely-tressed.
J. M. EDMONDS

Come to me, O ye graces,
Delicate, tender, fair;
Come from your heavenly places,
Muses with golden hair.   H. DE VERE STACKPOOLE

LXXV. ADONIS IS DYING

The delicate Adonis is dying, Cytherea; what can we do?
. . . Beat your breasts, maidens, and rend your garments.
EDMONDS 103

Delicate Adonis is dying, Cytherea; what shall we do?
Beat your breasts, maidens, and rend your tunics.
WHARTON 62

Gentle Adonis is dying, O Cythera; what shall we do?
Beat your breasts, O maidens, and rend your garments.
COX 59

Tender Adonis stricken is lying,
What, Cytherea, now can we do?
Beat your breasts, maidens, Adonis is dying,
Rending your garments, the white fragments strew.
       H. DE VERE STACKPOOLE

Gentle Adonis wounded lies, dying, dying.
What message, O Cythera, dost thou send?
Beat, beat your white breasts, O ye weeping maidens,
And in wild grief your mourning garments rend.
       EDWIN M. COX

LXXVI. SOFT GARMENTS

And wrapped her all about with cambric soft.
       EDMONDS 105

She wrapped herself well in delicate hairy ...
       WHARTON 89

She wrapped herself well in gossamer garments.
       COX 86

LXXVII. DELIGHT NOR PAIN

I will have neither honey nor bees ... EDMONDS 106

Neither honey nor bee for me. WHARTON 113

Oh, not the honey, nor the bee! MICHAEL FIELD

LXXVIII. FLOWERS

A MAIDEN full tender plucking flowers.   WHARTON *121*

A MOST tender maiden gathering flowers   COX *114*

I SAW one day a-gathering flowers
The daintiest little maid.   EDMONDS *107*

LXXIX. DYING, TO HER DAUGHTER

FOR lamentation may not be in a poet's house: such things befit not us.   WHARTON *136*

FOR it is not right that in the house of song there be mourning. Such things befit not us.   ROBINSON *155*

NAY, lamentation must not dwell
Within a poet's house ...   MICHAEL FIELD

NO HOUSE that serves the Muse hath room, I wis,
For grief; and so it ill beseemeth this.   EDMONDS *108*

LXXX. GOLD

GOLD is a child of Zeus; no moth nor worm devours it, and it overcomes the strongest of mortal hearts.

EDMONDS *110*

Yea, gold is son of Zeus: no rust
    Its timeless light can stain;
The worm that brings man's flesh to dust
    Assaults its strength in vain.   MICHAEL FIELD

LXXXI. THE MOON HAS SET

The moon has set, and the Pleiades; it is midnight, the time is going by, and I sleep alone.   WHARTON 52

The moon hath left the sky;
Lost is the Pleiads' light;
It is midnight
And time slips by;
But on my couch alone I lie.   J. ADDINGTON SYMONDS

The moon has set, and o'er the seas
Throw their last glance the Pleiades;
The weary night is waning fast,
The promised hour is come and past;—
Yet sleepless and alone I lie,
Alone—ah, false one, tell me why.   BLACKWOOD

The silver moon is set;
The Pleiades are gone;
Half the long night is spent, and yet
I lie alone.   JOHN H. MERIVALE

The moon has set beyond the seas,
And vanished are the Pleiades;
Half the long weary night has gone,
Time passes—yet I lie alone.   H. DE VERE STACKPOOLE

LXXXII. AS ROUND AN ALTAR

The moon rose full, and the maidens, taking their stand about the altar...   EDMONDS *112*

The moon rose full, and the women stood as though around an altar.   WHARTON *53*

The moon rose full: the women stood
As though within a sacred wood
Around an altar...   MICHAEL FIELD

Now rose the moon, full and argentine,
While round stood the maidens, as at a shrine.
      EDWIN M. COX

Then the full globèd moon arose, and there
The women stood as round an altar fair.
      H. DE VERE STACKPOOLE

LXXXIII. THE CRETAN WOMEN

Thus of old did the dainty feet of Cretan maidens dance pat to the music beside some lovely altar, pressing the soft smooth bloom of the grass.   EDMONDS *114*

Thus at times with tender feet the Cretan women dance in measure round the fair altar, trampling the fine soft bloom of the grass.   WHARTON *54*

THUS sometimes, the Cretan women, tender footed, dance in measure round the fair altar, crushing the fine bloom of the grass.   COX 50

THE Cretan women thus of old carefully with tender feet danced about a fair altar, treading the delicate soft bloom of the sward.   ROBINSON 25

AND thus at times, in Crete, the women there
Circle in dance around the altar fair;
In measured movement, treading as they pass
With tender feet the soft bloom of the grass.
                                        H. DE VERE STACKPOOLE

[With the previous]:

THEN, as the broad moon rose on high,
The maidens stood the altar nigh;
And some in graceful measure
The well-loved spot danced round,
With lightsome footsteps treading
The soft and grassy ground.   M. J. WALHOUSE

LXXXIV. MNASIDICA

MNASIDICA, of fairer form than the dainty Gyrinno.
                                                EDMONDS 115

MNASIDICA is more shapely than the tender Gyrinno.
                                                WHARTON 76

More shapely is Mnasidica, than gentle Gyrinno.
COX 73

Mnasidica of fairer shape than tenderest Gyrinno.
J. M. EDMONDS

LXXXV. GO GARLANDED

... But do you, Dica, let your dainty fingers twine a wreath of anise-sprays and bind your lovely locks; for it may well be that the blessed Graces, too, are more apt to look with favor on that which is adorned with flowers, whereas they turn away from all that goes ungarlanded...
EDMONDS 117

Do thou, Dica, surround garlands with fair foliage, with soft hands twining shoots of dill together: for even the blessèd Graces look kindlier on a flowery sacrifice, and turn their face away from those who lack garlands.
WHARTON 78

Do thou, O Dica, set garlands upon thy lovely hair, weaving sprigs of dill with thy delicate hands; for those who wear fair blossoms may surely stand first even in the presence of Goddesses who look without favor upon those who come ungarlanded.
COX 75

But place those garlands on thy lovely hair,
Twining the tender sprouts of anise green
With skilful hand; for offerings and flowers
Are pleasing to the Gods, who hate all those
Who come before them with uncrownèd heads.
C. D. YONGE

OF foliage and flowers love-laden
Twine wreaths for thy flowing hair,
With thine own soft fingers, maiden,
Weave garlands of parsley fair;
For flowers are sweet, and the Graces
On suppliants wreathed with may
Look down from their heavenly places,
But turn from the crownless away.　　J. A. SYMONDS

HERE, fairest Rhodope, recline,
And 'mid thy bright locks intertwine,
With fingers soft as softest down,
The ever verdant parsley crown.
The Gods are pleased with flowers that bloom
And leaves that shed divine perfume,
But, if ungarlanded, despise
The richest offered sacrifice.　　JOHN H. MERIVALE

LET dainty fingers, Dica mine,
With wreathen dill thy love-locks twine;
For that which is with flowers gay,
Favor never saith it nay.
But she will turn away her head
From all that goes ungarlanded.　　J. M. EDMONDS

WEAVE garlands, maiden, from the strands
Of dill, and with soft gentle hands
Set the delicious leafage round your head.

The Goddess and the happy Graces
Love to look on flower-crowned faces,
But turn aside from the ungarlanded.
C. M. BOWRA

Bring summer flowers, bring pansy, violet,
Moss-rose and sweet-briar and blue columbine,
Bring loveliest leaves, rathe privet, eglantine,
Brown myrtles with the dews of morning wet:
Twine thou a wreath upon thy brows to set;
With thy soft hands the wayward tendrils twine;
Then place them, maiden, on those curls of thine,
Those curls too fair for gems or coronet.
Sweet is the breath of blossoms, and the Graces,
When suppliants through Love's temple wend their way,
Look down with smiles from their celestial places
On maidens wreathed with chaplets of the may;
But from the crownless choir they hide their faces,
Nor heed them when they sing nor when they pray.
J. ADDINGTON SYMONDS

Take sprigs of anise fair
With soft hands twined,
And round thy bonny hair
A chaplet bind;
The Muse with smiles will bless
Thy blossoms gay,
While from the garlandless
She turns away.
T. G. TUCKER

LXXXVI. DELICACY

... But I love delicacy, and the bright and the beautiful belong for me to the desire of the sunlight...

EDMONDS 118

I love refinement and for me Love has the splendor and beauty of the sun.

COX 76

I have loved delicacy from childhood, and for me Love has the sun's splendor and beauty.   ROBINSON 104

ALL delicacy unto me is lovely, and for me,
O Love!
Thy wings are as the midday fire,
Thy splendor as the sun above.

H. DE VERE STACKPOOLE

LXXXVII. TO HER PUPILS

You dishonor the good gifts of the buxom Muses, children, when you say "We will crown you, dear Sappho, best player of the clear sweet lyre." Know you not that my skin is all wrinkled with age, my hair is turned from black to white, my teeth are but few remaining, and the legs can scarce carry the body you used once to join in the dance, to foot it as nimbly as the little fawns, nimblest of living things? Yet I cannot help it. Not even God himself can do what cannot be; and surely as starry Night follows rosy-armed Dawn and brings us darkness unto the ends of the earth, Death tracks everything living and catches it in the end, and even as he would not give his beloved wife to Orpheus, so he ever thinks to keep prisoner every woman that dies, for all he should let her follow the song and string of her spouse. But I, be it known, love soft living, and for me brightness and beauty belong to the desire of the sunlight; and therefore I shall not crawl away to my lair till that needs must be, but continue loved and loving with you. And now it is enough that I have your love, nor would I pray for more... EDMONDS 118A

LXXXVIII. TO HER PUPILS

You had crouched silent behind the great baytree, children, when I passed yesterday on my way to the town; and in a moment all was sweeter for me when I saw you. Ah, but I drank that draught with thirsty eyes! Aye, the women that went with me thought me suddenly become a silent fellow-wayfarer and heedless of my company, and sometimes I scarcely heard them; for a humming overwhelmed my ears and my poor dear spirit flew away with my wits. Such things, it seems, are of fate, and methought, gentle maidens, I would come and visit you, but alas! when I did you were too quick, and shut me out. Yet I saw a fair sight ere the door was shut, and the very clothes on your backs, being yours, thrilled me through.

EDMONDS 118B

LXXXIX. TO A DREAM

O DREAM, thou child of black Night, who comest ere break of dawn when the sweet God of Sleep hath not long to stay upon our eyelids, how dire the pangs of grief thou foretellest me should I dare to keep desire and ability apart! Yet I have hopes I shall not meet the lot thou bodest, but refuse nothing I wish for if the Gods but offer it me; for when I was a child I should never have been so dull as to disdain my dear mother's offer of a pretty toy. And I pray the Gods give me the opportunity to take what I long for now, seeing that I have done them all such honor in my songs and dances. EDMONDS 118C

XC. TO ALCAEUS

[Who said to Sappho: I fain would speak to you, but shame restrains me]

If your desire were of things good or fair, and your tongue were not mixing a draught of ill words, then would not shame possess your eye, but you would make your plea outright. EDMONDS *119*

Hadst thou felt desire for things good or noble, and had not thy tongue framed some evil speech, shame had not filled thine eyes, but thou hadst spoken honestly about it. WHARTON *28*

Hadst thou wished for things good or noble and had not thy tongue formed evil speech, shame would not have shown from thine eyes, but thou hadst spoken frankly about it. COX *26*

a. I fain would speak, I fain would tell,
But shame and fear my utterance quell.
s. If aught of good, if aught of fair
Thy tongue were laboring to declare,
Nor shame should dash thy glance, nor fear
Forbid thy suit to reach my ear. ANON.

a. Sweet violet-weaving Sappho, whose soft smile
My tongue should free,
Lo, I would speak, but shame holds me the while
I gaze on thee.
s. Hadst thou but felt desire of noble things,

Hadst not thy tongue proposed to speak no good,
Thy words had not been destitute of wings,
Nor shame thine eyes subdued.

H. DE VERE STACKPOOLE

A. Sappho of the violet tresses,
Gently smiling, pure as day,
There's something that my heart confesses,
But shame takes my speech away.
S. Were your desiring good and fair
And did your tongue no ill prepare,
Then had no shame possessed your sight,
But you had pled your plea outright.

J. M. EDMONDS

XCI. TO A HANDSOME MAN

Stand up, look me in the face as friend to friend, and unveil the charm that is in your eyes.   EDMONDS 120

Stand face to face, friend ... and unveil the grace in thine eyes.   WHARTON 29

Face me, my dear one ... and unveil the grace in thine eyes.   COX 27

Stand and unfold as friend to friend the grace
That's in those eyes, and look me in the face.

J. M. EDMONDS

Friend, face me so and raise
Unto my face thy face,
Unto mine eyes thy gaze,
Unto my soul its grace.   H. DE VERE STACKPOOLE

XCII. TO A RIVAL, IN IRONY

A very good day to a daughter of very many kings.
                                        EDMONDS 121

All joy to thee, daughter of Polyanax.   WHARTON 86

From me all joy to thee, O daughter of Polyanax.
                                        COX 83

XCIII. SPRING RETURNS

Why does the heavenly swallow, daughter of Pandion,
vex me . . . ?   EDMONDS 122

Why, lovely swallow, Pandion's child, dost thou weary
me?   COX 85

Ah, Procne, wherefore dost thou weary me . . .
                            MICHAEL FIELD

Why am I vexed to see Pandion's child
The heavenly Swallow bring her gift of Spring?
                            J. M. EDMONDS

XCIV. A DREAM

I DREAMT that I talked with the Cyprus-born...
EDMONDS 123

IN a dream I spake with the daughter of Cyprus.
WHARTON 87

IN my dream, I spoke to the Cyprian goddess. COX 84

XCV. SLEEP

MAY you sleep in the bosom of a tender comrade...
EDMONDS 128

SLEEP thou in the bosom of thy tender girl-friend.
WHARTON 83

UPON thy girl friend's white and tender breast,
Sleep thou, and on her bosom find thy rest.
H. DE VERE STACKPOOLE

XCVI. COME YE MUSES

O COME hither, ye Muses, from your golden house...
EDMONDS 129

HITHER now, ye Muses, leaving golden surroundings.
COX 81

HITHER now, Muses! leaving golden seats...
MICHAEL FIELD

XCVII. CLEIS

I HAVE a pretty little daughter who looks like a golden flower, my darling Cleis, for whom I would not take all Lydia, nay nor lovely Lesbos. EDMONDS 130

I HAVE a fair daughter with a form like a golden flower, Cleis, the belovèd, above whom I prize nor all Lydia nor lovely Lesbos... WHARTON 85

I HAVE a fair daughter with a form like golden flowers, Cleis the belovedest whom I cherish more than all Lydia or lovely Lesbos. COX 82

I HAVE a child, a lovely one,
In beauty like the golden sun
Or like sweet flowers of earliest bloom;
And Cleis is her name, for whom
I Lydia's treasures, were they mine,
Would glad resign. JOHN H. MERIVALE

I HAVE a child; so fair
As golden flowers is she,
My Cleis, all my care.
I'd not give her away
For Lydia's wide sway
Nor lands men long to see. C. M. BOWRA

I HAVE a little daughter rare
That's like the golden flowers fair,
    My Cleis;

I would not take all Lydia wide
No, nor lovely Greece beside
    For Cleis.   J. M. EDMONDS

A FAIR daughter have I, Cleis by name
Like a golden flower she seems to me.
Far more than all Lydia her do I love,
Or Lesbos shimmering in the sea.   EDWIN M. COX

XCVIII. THE SPRING

THE many-garlanded earth puts on her broidery.
EDMONDS 133

THE much-wreathèd earth puts on her broidery.
ROBINSON 97

XCIX. I CANNOT WEAVE

SWEET mother, I truly cannot weave my web; for I am o'erwhelmed through Aphrodite with love of a slender youth.   EDMONDS 135

SWEET mother, I cannot weave my web, broken as I am by longing for a maiden, at soft Aphrodite's will.
WHARTON 90

MY sweet mother, broken by soft Aphrodite's spell, longing for a youth, I can no more weave the cloth.   COX 87

Oh, my sweet mother, 'tis in vain,
I cannot weave as once I wove,
So 'wildered is my heart and brain
With thinking of that youth I love. THOMAS MOORE

Sweet mother, let the weaving be,
My hand is faint to move.
Frail Aphrodite masters me;
I long for my young love. T. F. HIGHAM

My sweet mother! Fair Aphrodite's spell
Has from me sense and reason all bereft,
And, yearning for that dear belovèd youth,
No longer can I see the warp or weft. EDWIN M. COX

Sweet mother, at the idle loom I lean,
Weary with longing for the boy that still
Remains a dream of loveliness—to fill
My soul, my life, at Aphrodite's will.
  H. DE VERE STACKPOOLE

C. GUARD THY TONGUE

When anger swells in the heart, restrain the idly-barking tongue. EDMONDS 137

When anger spreads through the breast, guard thy tongue from barking idly. WHARTON 27

When anger surges through thy heart
Let not thy foolish tongue take part.   EDWIN M. COX

When anger stirs thy breast, speak not at all,
For words, once spoken, rest beyond recall.
H. DE VERE STACKPOOLE

CI. THE NIGHTINGALE

The lovely-voiced harbinger of Spring, the nightingale.
EDMONDS 138

Spring's messenger, the sweet-voiced nightingale.
WHARTON 39

The messenger of Spring, the sweet-voiced nightingale.
COX 37

The dear good angel of the spring
The nightingale.   BEN JONSON

Spring's messenger we hail,
The sweet-voiced nightingale.   MICHAEL FIELD

CII. GOLDEN PULSE

And golden pulses grew upon the shore.   EDMONDS 139

99

AND golden pulse grew along the shores.   COX 28

... GREW golden pulse along the sand.   MICHAEL FIELD

CIII. SLEEP

AND night's black slumber was shed upon their eyes.
EDMONDS 141

WHEN all night long sleep holds their eyes.
WHARTON 43

WHEN all night long sleep holds them.   COX 41

AND night's black slumber fell upon their eyes.
J. M. EDMONDS

CIV. LIKE A CHILD

AND I have flown to you like a child to its mother.
EDMONDS 142

AND I flutter like a child after her mother.   WHARTON 38

So, like a child after its mother, I flutter.   COX 36

LIKE a child whose mother's lost,
I am fluttering, terror-tossed.   M. J. WALHOUSE

CV. ON A CHILD'S TOMB

I AM a little maid who cannot talk, but yet, if I am asked a question, I say plain enough with the voice that never wearies of speech at my feet: I was dedicated to the Aethopian Child of Leto by Aristo daughter of Hermocleitus son of Saunaidas, a ministrant, thou Lady of women, of thine; to whom in gratitude bound be thou gracious, and give our family good fame.   EDMONDS 143

MAIDENS, dumb as I am I speak thus, if any ask, and set before your feet a tireless voice: To Leto's daughter Aethopia was I dedicated by Arista daughter of Hermocleides son of Saynaiades, thy servant, O queen of women; whom bless thou, and deign to glorify our house.
                                                            WHARTON 118

MAIDENS, though I am dumb, yet thus I speak, if any ask, and place at your feet one with an untiring voice: To Aethopia the daughter of Leto was I consecrated by Arista, daughter of Hermocleides Saonaiades, thy servant, O queen of women; whom mayest thou bless and deign to glorify our house. COX 112

VOICELESS I speak, and from the tomb reply,
Unto Aethopia, Leto's child, was I
Vowed by the daughter of Hermocleides,
Who was the son of Saonaiades.
O virgin queen, unto my prayer incline,
Bless him and cast thy blessing on our line.
H. DE VERE STACKPOOLE

CVI. ON TIMAS

THIS is the dust of Timas, who was received into Persephone's black chamber all unwed, and for whose death all her fair companions took knife and shore the lovely hair of their heads. EDMONDS 144

THIS is the dust of Timas, whom Persephone's dark chamber received, dead before her wedding; when she perished, all her fellows dressed with sharpened steel the lovely tresses of their heads. WHARTON 119

THIS is the dust of Timas whom the dark chamber of Persephone received, dead before her wedding; when she died all her companions clipped with sharpened metal all their lovely tresses. COX 113

This dust was Timas'; ere her bridal hour
She lies in Proserpina's gloomy bower;
Her virgin playmates from each lovely head
Cut with sharp steel their locks, the strewments for the
   dead.   CHARLES A. ELTON

This is the dust of Timas, whom unwed
Persephone locked in her darksome bed:
For her the maids who were her fellows shore
Their curls and to her tomb this tribute bore.
         J. A. SYMONDS

Here rests the dust of Timas who, unwed,
Passed the dark portals of Persephone.
With sharpened metal, when her spirit fled,
Her mourning friends each shore her fair-tressed head.
         EDWIN M. COX

This is the dust of Timas, who, unwed,
Passed hence to Proserpina's house of gloom;
In mourning all her sorrowing playmates shed
Their curls and cast the tribute on her tomb.
       H. DE VERE STACKPOOLE

CVII. THE FISHERMAN'S TOMB

To the fisherman Pelagon his father Meniscus has put up a fishing-basket and an oar as a memorial of his hard life.
        EDMONDS 145

Over the fisherman Pelagon his father Meniscus sets weel and oar, memorial of a luckless life.   WHARTON 120

This oar and net and fisher's wickered snare
Meniscus placed above his buried son—
Memorials of the lot in life he bore,
The hard and needy life of Pelagon.   CHARLES A. ELTON

Here, to the fisher Pelagon, his sire Meniscus laid
A wicker-net and oar, to show his weary life and trade.
LORD NEAVES

Over the fisher Pelagon Meniscus his father set
The oar worn by the wave, the trap, and the fishing net;
For all men, and for ever, memorials there to be
Of the luckless life of the fisher, the laborer of the sea.
H. DE VERE STACKPOOLE

CVIII. THE GOD'S TOAST

There stood a mixing-bowl of ambrosia ready mixed, and Hermes took the wine-jug to pour out for the Gods. And then they all took up the beakers, and pouring a libation wished all manner of good luck to the bridegroom.
EDMONDS 146

And there the bowl of ambrosia was mixed, and Hermes took the ladle to pour out for the gods; and then they all held goblets, and made libation, and wished the bridegroom all good luck.   WHARTON 51

And with ambrosia the crater was mixed; and Hermes seized the ladle to pour out for the gods; and they all lifted up their beakers and poured libation and prayed for all blessings for the bridegroom.   ROBINSON *129*

The ambrosia-bowl stood mingled on the board,
And Hermes took the jug each cup to fill,
And all the Gods raised cups, and offerings poured,
Wishing the bridegroom well with right good will.
J. M. EDMONDS

Ambrosia there was mixed, and from his station
Hermes the bowl for waiting gods outpoured;
Then raised they all their cups and made libation,
Blessing the bridegroom by the bride adored.
H. DE VERE STACKPOOLE

CVIX. TO THE BRIDE

Bride that teemest with rosy desires, bride the fairest ornament of the Queen of Paphos, hie thee to bed, hie thee to the couch whereon thou must sweetly sport in gentle wise with thy bridegroom. And may the Star of Eve lead thee full willingly to the place where thou shalt marvel at the silver-thronèd Lady of Wedlock.

EDMONDS *147*

Bride, teeming with rosy loves, bride, fairest image of the goddess of Paphos, go to the couch, go to the bed, softly sporting, sweet to the bridegroom. May Hesperus lead thee rejoicing, honoring Hera of the silver throne, goddess of marriage. WHARTON 133

BRIDE, teeming with rosy loves, bride the fairest image of the Paphian goddess, hie thee to the bed, hie thee to the couch, softly sporting, sweet to thy bridegroom. May Hesperus, the evening star, lead thee willingly where thou shalt marvel at Hera of the silver throne, goddess of wedlock. ROBINSON 145

BRIDE, in whose breast haunt rosy loves!
Bride, fairest of the Paphian groves!
Hence, to thy marriage rise, and go!
Hence to the bed, where thou shalt show
With honeyed play thy wedded charms,
Thy sweetness in the bridegroom's arms!
Let Hesper lead thee forth, a wife,
Willing and worshipping for life,
The silver-throned, the wedlock dame,
Queen Hera, wanton without shame!
J. ADDINGTON SYMONDS

BRIDE, around whom the rosy loves are flying,
Sweet image of the Cyprian undying,
The bed awaits thee; go, and with him lying,
Give to the groom thy sweetness, softly sighing.
May Hesperus in gladness pass before thee,
And Hera of the silver throne bend o'er thee.
H. DE VERE STACKPOOLE

CX. WEDDING SONG

RAISE high the roof-beam, carpenters. Hymenaeus! Like Ares comes the bridegroom, Hymenaeus! taller far than a tall man. Hymenaeus! **WHARTON 91**

UP with the rafters high, Ho for the wedding!
Raise them high, ye joiners, Ho for the wedding!
The bridegroom's as tall as Ares, Ho for the wedding!
Far taller than a tall man, Ho for the wedding!
Towering as the Lesbian poet, Ho for the wedding!
Over the poets of other lands, Ho for the wedding!
  EDMONDS 148

RAISE high the roof beams, workmen! Hymenaeus!
Like Ares comes the bridegroom! Hymenaeus!
Taller far than all tall men! Hymenaeus! **COX 88**

ARTISTS, raise the rafters high!
Ample scope and stately plan—
Mars-like comes the bridegroom night,
Loftier than a lofty man. **ANON.**

WORKMEN lift high the beams of the roof,
Hymenaeus!
Like Ares from sky comes the groom to the bride,
Hymenaeus!
Than men who must die stands he taller in pride,
Hymenaeus! **H. DE VERE STACKPOOLE**

CXI. THE EVENING STAR

Evening Star that bringest back all that lightsome Dawn hath scattered afar, thou bringest the sheep, thou bringest the goat, thou bringest her child home to the mother . . .
EDMONDS 149

Evening, thou bringest all that bright morning scattered, thou bringest the sheep, the goat, and the child back to its mother.
COX 92

O Hesperus! Thou bringest all things home;
All that the garish day hath scattered wide;
The sheep, the goat, back to the welcome fold;
Thou bring'st the child, too, to his mother's side.
APPLETON

Thou, Hesper, bringest homeward all
That radiant dawn sped far and wide,
The sheep to fold, the goat to stall,
The children to their mother's side.
RENNELL RODD

Star that bringest home again
All bright Dawn spreads far and wide,
Goat to fold and sheep to pen,
And children to their mother's side.
J. M. EDMONDS

Hail, gentle Evening, that bringest back
All things that bright morning hath beguiled.
Thou bringest the lamb, thou bringest the kid,
And to its mother her drowsy child.
EDWIN M. COX

CHILDREN astray to their mothers,
    and goats to the herd,
Sheep to the shepherd, through
    twilight the wings of the bird,
All things that morning has scattered
    with fingers of gold,
All things thou bringest, O Evening!
    at last to the fold.
H. DE VERE STACKPOOLE

O HESPERUS, thou bringest all good things—
Home to the weary, to the hungry cheer,
To the young bird the parent's brooding wings,
The welcome stall to the o'erlabored steer;
Whate'er of peace about our hearthstone clings,
Whate'er our household gods protect of dear,
Are gathered round us by thy look of rest;
Thou bring'st the child too to its mother's breast.
LORD BYRON

[See also number XXI]

CXII. LIKE THE APPLE

As the sweet-apple blushes on the end of the bough, the very end of the bough, which the gatherers overlooked, nay overlooked not but could not reach.   WHARTON 93

As the sweet apple blushes on the end of the bough, the very end of the bough which the gatherers missed, nay missed not, but could not reach.   COX 90

At the end of the bough—its uttermost end,
Missed by the harvesters, ripens the apple,
Nay, not overlooked, but far out of their reach,
     So with all best things.   EDWIN M. COX

Like the sweet apple that reddens
At end of the bough—far end of the bough—
Left by the gatherers swaying, forgotten, so thou.
Nay, not forgotten, ungotten, ungathered till now.
     H. DE VERE STACKPOOLE

CXIII. LIKE THE HYACINTH

Like the hyacinth which the shepherd tramples underfoot on the mountain, and it still blooms purple on the ground.
     EDMONDS *151*

As on the hills the shepherds trample the hyacinth under foot and the purple flower is pressed to earth.
     WHARTON *94*

As on the hills, the shepherds trample the larkspur under foot and the flower lies empurpling in decay on the ground.
     COX *91*

O'er the hills the heedless shepherd,
Heavy footed, plods his way;
Crushed behind him lies the larkspur,
Soon empurpling in decay.   EDWIN M. COX

As on the hills the shepherds
Trample the hyacinth down,
Staining the earth with darkness,
There where a flower has blown.

H. DE VERE STACKPOOLE

[With the previous]:

LIKE the sweet apple which reddens upon the topmost
    bough,
A-top on the topmost twig,—which the pluckers forgot
    somehow,—
Forgot it not, nay, but got it not, for none could get it till
    now.

LIKE the wild hyacinth flower, which on the hill is found,
Which the passing feet of the shepherds for ever tear and
    wound,
Until the purple blossom is trodden into the ground.

D. G. ROSSETTI

CXIV. THE DOORKEEPER'S FEET

THE doorkeeper's feet are seven fathoms long, and his sandals five hides to the pair—it took ten shoemakers to make them; and his father lived in other ways an honest life, but claimed to be better born than Cecrops himself.

EDMONDS 154

To the doorkeeper feet seven fathoms long, and sandals of five bulls' hides, the work of ten cobblers. WHARTON 98

Master Doorkeeper's pretty feet
Twelve good ells long must be;
It takes five hides to make his shoes,
And cobblers three times three.   J. M. EDMONDS

CXV. HAPPY BRIDEGROOM

Happy bridegroom, the marriage is accomplished as you prayed it should be, and the maiden you prayed for is yours ... and soft and gentle is shed over her delightsome face ...   EDMONDS *155*

Happy bridegroom, now is thy wedding come to thy desire, and thou hast the maiden of thy desire ... and a hue of honey-paleness overspreads the lovely countenance.
    WHARTON *99, 100*

Happy bridegroom, now has come thy wedding as thou wished, and thou hast the maiden of thy desire ... and a sweet expression spreads over her fair face.   COX *96, 97*

Thou happy bridegroom! Now has dawned
That day of days supreme,
When in thine arms thou'lt hold at last
The maiden of thy dream.   EDWIN M. COX

Joy born of marriage thou provest,
Bridegroom thrice blest,
Holding the maiden thou lovest
Clasped to thy breast.   H. DE VERE STACKPOOLE

CXVI. O BEAUTEOUS ONE

O beauteous one, O lovely one, thine it is to sport with the rose-ankled Graces and Aphrodite the golden . . .
EDMONDS 157

O beautiful, O charming one, with thee sport the rosy-ankled Graces and golden Aphrodite. ROBINSON 139

CXVII. CAN IT BE

Can it be that I still long for my virginity?
EDMONDS 159

Do I still long for maidenhood? WHARTON 102

CXVIII. TO A BRIDE

Thy form, O bride, is all delight; thy eyes are of a gentle hue; thy fair face is overspread with love; Aphrodite hath done thee exceeding honor. EDMONDS 158

Graceful is thy form, and thine eyes are of a soft hue, O bride, and love has been poured over thy fair face; and thou hast been honored preeminently by Aphrodite.
ROBINSON 140

Thy form is lovely and thine eyes are honeyed,
O'er thy face the pale
Clear light of love lies like a veil.

Bidding thee rise, with outstretched hands,
Before thee Aphrodite stands.

H. DE VERE STACKPOOLE

CXIX. TO THE BRIDEGROOM

To what, dear bridegroom, may I well liken thee? To a slender sapling do I best liken thee.   EDMONDS *161*

Whereunto may I well liken thee, dear bridegroom? To a soft shoot may I best liken thee.   WHARTON *104*

To what may I liken thee, dear bridegroom? Best to a tender shoot may I liken thee.   COX *101*

Bridegroom dear, to what shall I compare thee? To a slim green rod best do I compare thee.   ANON.

CXX. TO THE BRIDEGROOM

For never, bridegroom, was there another maiden such as this.   EDMONDS *163*

For there was no other girl, O bridegroom, like her.   WHARTON *106*

For, like her, O bridegroom, there was no other maiden.   COX *103*

CXXI. TO HER VIRGINITY

MAIDENHOOD, maidenhood, whither art thou gone from me? . . . Never again will I come to thee, never again.
WHARTON 109

MAIDENHOOD, maidenhood, whither art thou gone from me? . . . Never, O never again shall I return to thee.
COX 104

MAIDENHEAD, maidenhead, whither away?
Where I must stay, bride, where I must stay.
EDMONDS 164

MAIDENHOOD! Maidenhood! where
    hast thou gone from me,
Whither, O Slain?
I shall return to thee, I who have
    gone from thee, never again.
H. DE VERE STACKPOOLE

CXXII. THOU HAST CHOSEN

MICA wishes to bring thee here but I shall not allow thee. Thou hast chosen friendship with the daughters of the house of Penthilus, O mischievous one! . . . For us sings the soft-voiced poet a sweet song and the clear-voiced nightingales . . . and the dewy leaves . . . ROBINSON 194

CXXIII. OLD AGE

... Brings advance to the features of the face ... beautiful gifts, children ... O friend, the singer of shrill lyres all flesh old age already ... and the hairs have become white from black ... and the knees do not carry ...

ROBINSON *203*

CXXIV. O DREAM

O dream with black wings, mayest thou come when sleep brings forgetfulness ... Sweet is the god. Terribly thou dost afflict me ...

ROBINSON *198*

THIS TEXT IS SET IN THE
ESTIENNE TYPES
AND PRINTED ON A PAPER
MADE SPECIALLY FOR
THE PETER PAUPER PRESS